Julie Stephani's

Ultimate

Scrapbook

GUIDE

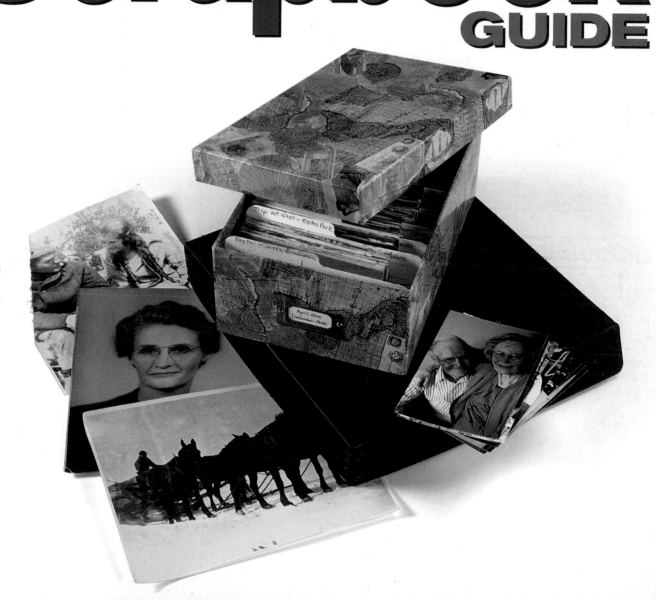

From The Television Series *More Than Memories*

Compiled and Edited by Julie Stephani

Graphic Design
Jon Stein

Photography
Kris Kandler
Robert Best

Published by
Krause Publications
700 East State Street
Iola, WI 54990-0001
Telephone (715) 445-2214
www.krause.com

Please call or write for our free catalog of publications.
Our toll-free number to place an order or obtain a free catalog is (800) 258-0929
or please use our regular business telephone (715) 445-2214
for editorial comment and further information.

Library of Congress Catalog Card Number: 2001086368

ISBN 0-87349-287-0

Manufactured in the United States of America

The content of this book is based on the *More Than Memories* television series.

Introduction

Scrapbooking is an opportunity to keep your treasured family memories alive. Organizing and displaying your photos on creative pages in albums will be time that will bring you great pleasure. Each grouping of photos will capture your special memories to enjoy again and again. It is your family history that will be treasured by future generations as well.

Some of my most valuable possessions are the photos and journals of my ancestors. They probably did not think they were documenting our family history when they wrote about their everyday experiences, but today I have a glimpse of who they were and how they lived as they crossed the prairies to establish homesteads for their families. It gives me a sense of my family roots.

We have the opportunity to collect our memories in scrapbooks today that will be a part of our family history for future generations. It will give them a glimpse of who we were and how we lived in the 20th and 21st centuries.

Begin today. This book will help you through the steps of organizing your photos and memorabilia and will give you many tips and techniques for displaying your memories in creative ways. This may be one of the most rewarding things you ever do for yourself and your family. Take the time to enjoy each part of the scrapbooking experience.

More Than Memories Sponsors

The following manufacturers' products and publishers' materials have been used to create the sample pages in this book.

Accu-Cut Shape and Letter Cutting Systems®
www.accucut.com

Creating Keepsakes™ Scrapbook Magazine
www.creatingkeepsakes.com

Delta Technical Coatings, Inc.
www.DeltaCrafts.com

Eastman Kodak Company
Kodak.com

EK Success Ltd.
www.eksuccess.com

Epson America, Inc.
Epson.com

Fiskars®, Inc.
www.fiskars.com

Hot Off The Press, Inc.
www.hotp.com

JANGLE™
www.JANGLE.com

Krause Publications
www.krause.com

3L® Corporation
www.3Lcorp.com

Memory Makers Magazine
www.memorymakermagazine.com

Pioneer® E-Z Load Memory Albums
www.pioneerphotoalbums.com

◆ ◆ ◆ contents ◆ ◆ ◆

◆ ◆ ◆ beginning ◆ ◆ ◆

Where Do I Start?

Seven
Easy Steps

Collect, organize, and
store photos safely.

1 Organize and Preserve Photos
Collect and sort your photos, negatives, and memorabilia. Store them in photo-safe containers.

2 Buy and Organize Supplies
Begin with the basics. Add supplies to fit your personal needs.

3 Choose Themes and Select Photos
Group photos into themes, subjects, or events.

4 Crop and Mat Photos
Decide on the size and shape of your photos. Frame them with paper mats.

5 Lay out Pages
Arrange photos, memorabilia, and design elements on your scrapbook pages.

6 Journal on Pages
Tell the facts, describe details, or tell the rest of the story. How much information to include is up to you.

7 Protect and Collect Pages
Place completed pages in protective plastic sleeves and collect them in an album.

Organize Photos
Gather all of your photos in one area where you can work undisturbed. It will probably take several sittings before you have sorted through your collection. Decide how to group your photos and place them in piles. Most scrapbookers group them chronologically by years. Older pictures may be grouped by families. You may find it helpful to group photos based on different stages or turning points in your life such as childhood, school years, after marriage, etc.

Once you have your photos sorted, store them in photo-safe containers. Even though you will want to save all of your photos for historical value, you will probably be selective when it comes to choosing what goes into your albums. Photo boxes are good storage containers, and labeled index cards will help you find photos easily.

Organize Negatives

Collect and sort your negatives in the same way as you do your photos. One of the best methods for storing and retrieving negatives is to organize them in chronological order and label them by events. Protect them in photo-safe plastic sleeves or envelopes and store them in boxes or albums.

Store negatives and photos separately so you will have a back-up if one or the other is accidentally damaged or destroyed.

Develop a Plan

How do you want to approach scrapbooking? Do you want to display all of your current photos on creative pages or will you only work on special-event pages? What will you do with the photos that don't go in your special albums? Are you going to begin with your heritage photos from the past or with your most recent photographs?

How ever you decide to begin, it is wise to start with a smaller project that is not overwhelming. Store the photos and negatives you won't be using in a safe place. You have already accomplished a lot simply by getting them organized!

The method I have used over the years is to place my photos in albums with plastic pocket sleeves as soon as I get them processed. That way, I have all of my photos in chronological order and it is a pictorial family history of the events in our lives. Sometimes I place an inferior or similar photo behind another one. Photos are numbered and a journaling index is included with each album. I use the second prints or make reprints for my special scrapbook pages.

I do something different for business photos, which I take often at events in my travels. These photos are placed in photo file boxes and labeled by event, date, and location. I include postcards to identify all of the places I've been. I store business photos differently because they are not looked at as often as my personal photos, and I also take so many pictures that I would have too many albums to store.

◆◆◆ supplies ◆◆◆

What Basic Supplies Do I Need?

There are many scrapbooking supplies available. Begin with the basics and add supplies as you determine your needs.

Album   **Scissors**
Paper   **Pen**
Pencil   **Ruler**
Adhesive
Protective Plastic Sleeves

How Do I Choose the Right Album?

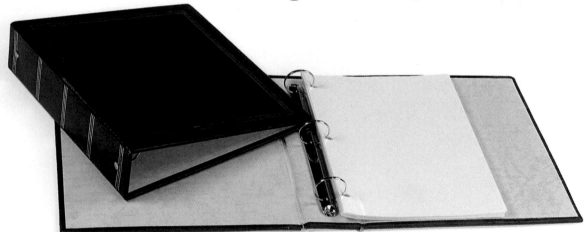

Album Styles

Photos should be stored in "archival quality" albums to preserve them over the years. Albums come in a variety of sizes with different bindings and cover materials. Choose different albums to fit your different needs.

Albums range from small 2" x 3" mini albums to 12" x 15." The albums most commonly used are 8½" x 11" and 12" x 12." The size you choose depends on the photos and memorabilia that you want to include inside. Background papers can be cut to size or can be expanded with some clever piecing.

Three-Ring Bound

Background paper is inserted in top-loading plastic protective sleeves that have holes to fit the rings. Some three-ring binders have "D" shaped rings, which allow pages to lie flat. The rings open easily for additions or changes in how pages are arranged.

◆ ◆ ◆ supplies ◆ ◆ ◆

Spiral Bound

The number of pages is fixed, not allowing for additions or changes in page arrangement. They work well for special theme or gift albums. Protective sleeves are not always included. Pages lie flat when open.

Post Bound

Screws in the binding allow for additions or changes in page arrangement. Additional refills and protective sleeves are sold separately. Extension posts can increase the depth of the album to hold additional pages.

Strap Bound

Plastic straps woven through sturdy staples and attached to the pages allow the pages to lie flat. Protective sleeves can be removed while working on pages and then can be replaced. The facing pages lie close together, which works well for two-page spreads and pop-up pages.

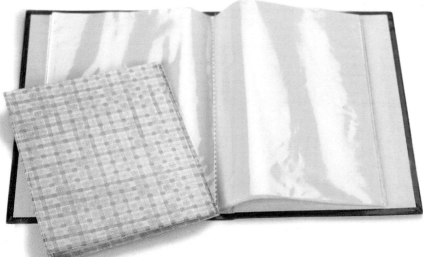

Stitch Bound

The number of pages is fixed, not allowing for additions or changes in page arrangement. They work well for special theme or gift albums.

◆◆◆ supplies ◆◆◆

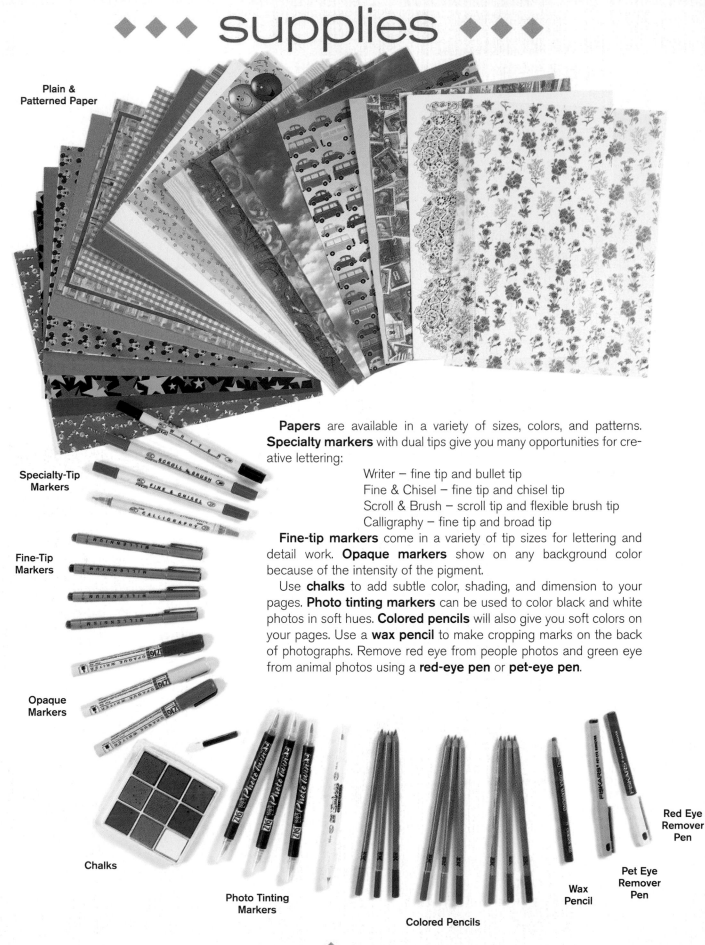

Plain & Patterned Paper

Specialty-Tip Markers

Fine-Tip Markers

Opaque Markers

Chalks

Photo Tinting Markers

Colored Pencils

Wax Pencil

Pet Eye Remover Pen

Red Eye Remover Pen

Papers are available in a variety of sizes, colors, and patterns. **Specialty markers** with dual tips give you many opportunities for creative lettering:

        Writer – fine tip and bullet tip
        Fine & Chisel – fine tip and chisel tip
        Scroll & Brush – scroll tip and flexible brush tip
        Calligraphy – fine tip and broad tip

Fine-tip markers come in a variety of tip sizes for lettering and detail work. **Opaque markers** show on any background color because of the intensity of the pigment.

Use **chalks** to add subtle color, shading, and dimension to your pages. **Photo tinting markers** can be used to color black and white photos in soft hues. **Colored pencils** will also give you soft colors on your pages. Use a **wax pencil** to make cropping marks on the back of photographs. Remove red eye from people photos and green eye from animal photos using a **red-eye pen** or **pet-eye pen**.

◆ ◆ ◆ supplies ◆ ◆ ◆

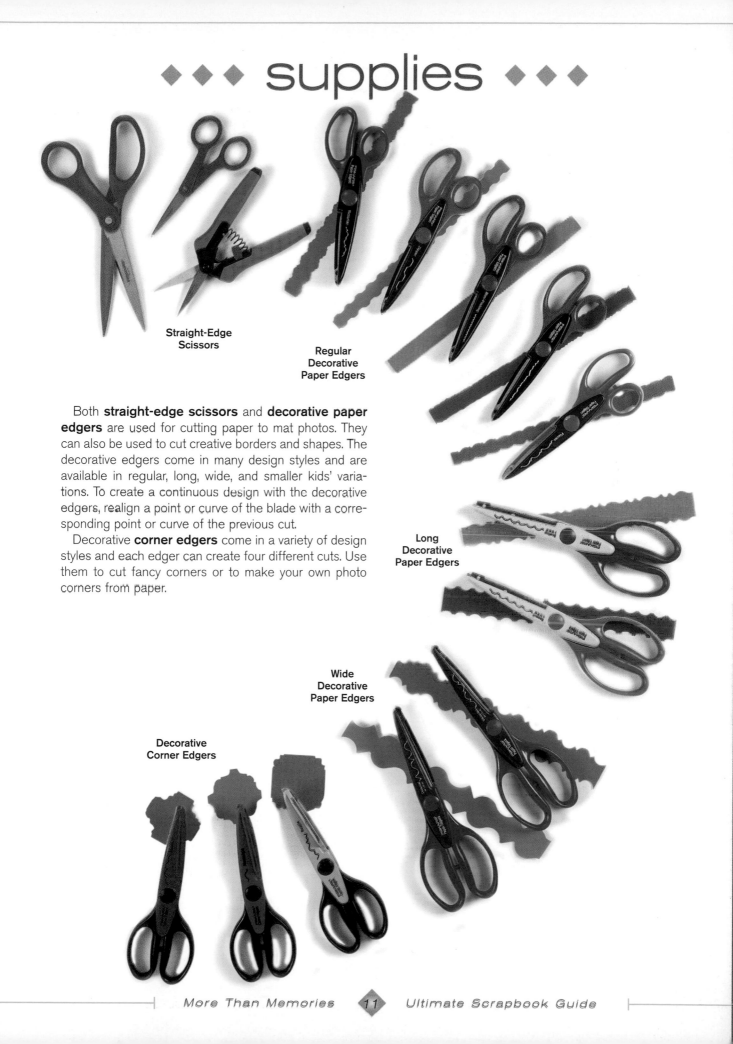

Straight-Edge Scissors

Regular Decorative Paper Edgers

Long Decorative Paper Edgers

Wide Decorative Paper Edgers

Decorative Corner Edgers

Both **straight-edge scissors** and **decorative paper edgers** are used for cutting paper to mat photos. They can also be used to cut creative borders and shapes. The decorative edgers come in many design styles and are available in regular, long, wide, and smaller kids' variations. To create a continuous design with the decorative edgers, realign a point or curve of the blade with a corresponding point or curve of the previous cut.

Decorative **corner edgers** come in a variety of design styles and each edger can create four different cuts. Use them to cut fancy corners or to make your own photo corners from paper.

◆◆◆ supplies ◆◆ ◆

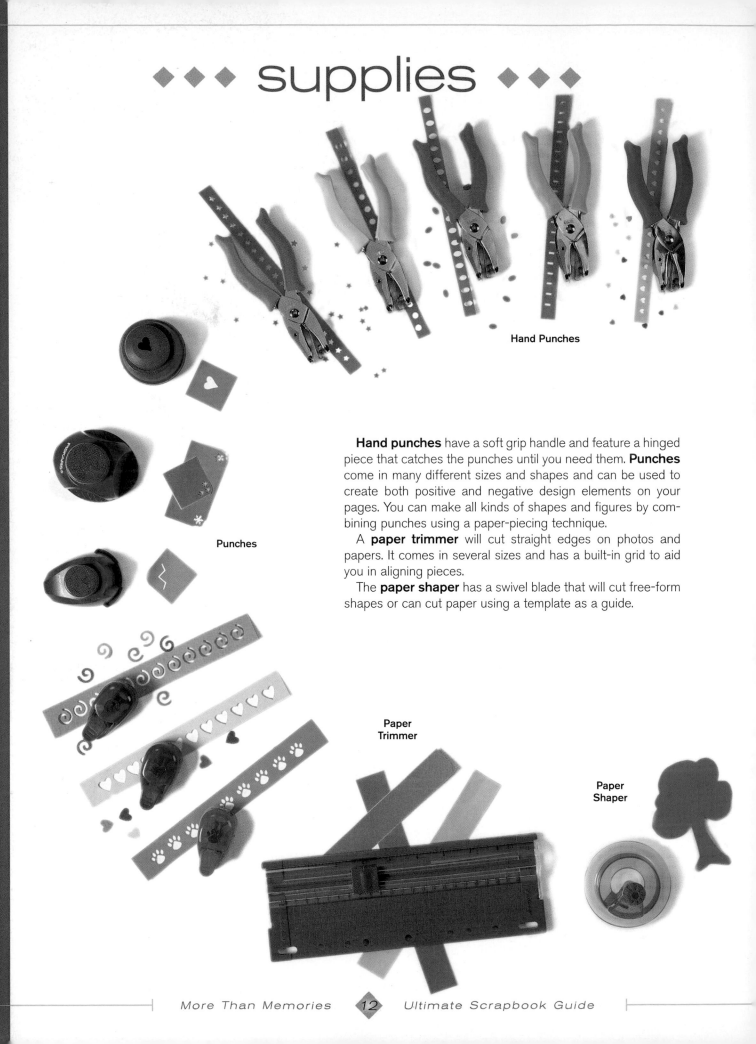

Hand Punches

Punches

Hand punches have a soft grip handle and feature a hinged piece that catches the punches until you need them. **Punches** come in many different sizes and shapes and can be used to create both positive and negative design elements on your pages. You can make all kinds of shapes and figures by combining punches using a paper-piecing technique.

A **paper trimmer** will cut straight edges on photos and papers. It comes in several sizes and has a built-in grid to aid you in aligning pieces.

The **paper shaper** has a swivel blade that will cut free-form shapes or can cut paper using a template as a guide.

Paper Trimmer

Paper Shaper

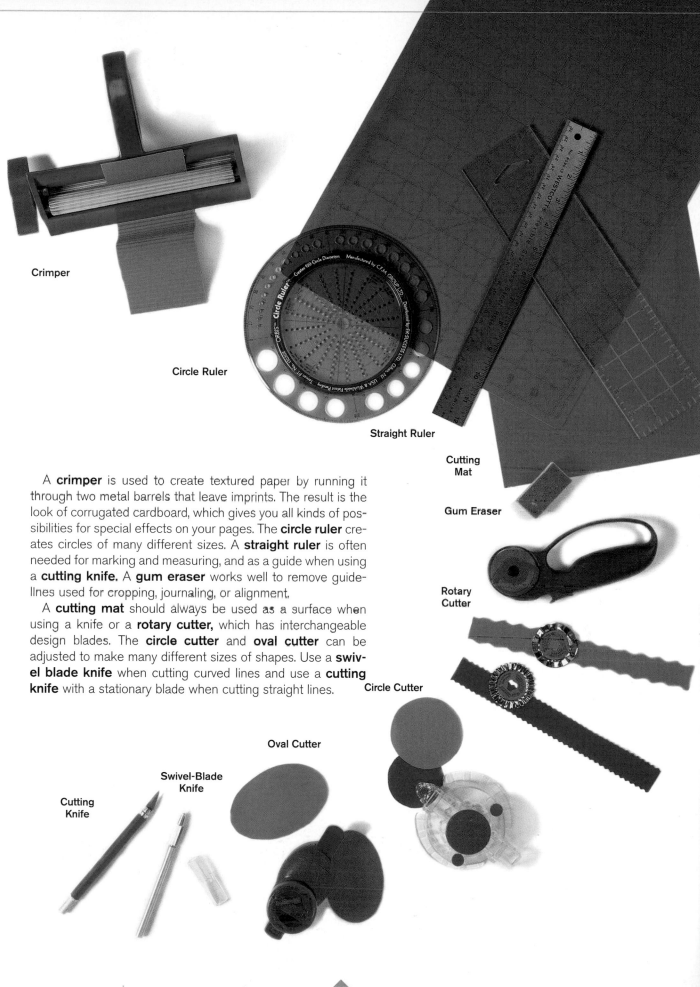

Crimper

Circle Ruler

Straight Ruler

Cutting Mat

Gum Eraser

Rotary Cutter

Circle Cutter

Oval Cutter

Swivel-Blade Knife

Cutting Knife

A **crimper** is used to create textured paper by running it through two metal barrels that leave imprints. The result is the look of corrugated cardboard, which gives you all kinds of possibilities for special effects on your pages. The **circle ruler** creates circles of many different sizes. A **straight ruler** is often needed for marking and measuring, and as a guide when using a **cutting knife.** A **gum eraser** works well to remove guidelines used for cropping, journaling, or alignment.

A **cutting mat** should always be used as a surface when using a knife or a **rotary cutter,** which has interchangeable design blades. The **circle cutter** and **oval cutter** can be adjusted to make many different sizes of shapes. Use a **swivel blade knife** when cutting curved lines and use a **cutting knife** with a stationary blade when cutting straight lines.

Adhesive Foam Dots

Mounting Tape

Photo Stickers

Photo Stickers 500 pcs.

Photo Corners 250 pcs.

Photo Corners

Adhesives

Stencils & Templates

Paper Paint

◆ supplies ◆

Photo corners can be used for decorative purposes or when you want to attach a photo that you may want to remove. **Photo stickers** are small adhesive tabs that can be used in place of glue. **Mounting tape** and **adhesive foam dots** are two-sided adhesives with a layer of foam in between. They can be used to add dimension to items on the page. Use **adhesives** that are acid-free.

Stencils or **templates** are tracing guides used to create shapes, letters, numbers, and borders. Use acid-free **paper paint** when stenciling on your pages. **Die-cuts** come in hundreds of shapes and sizes. Pre-cut die-cuts are usually grouped by themes.

Die-Cuts

Punch-Outs

◆ supplies ◆

Punch-Outs come in many different shapes, but they also come in frames, photo corners, and borders. They do not have any adhesive so you can move them around on your page until you have them in the perfect place. They have a white border, which separates them from color or patterned paper and makes them "pop" out on the page.

There are hundreds of **stickers** from which to choose. They are a quick way to add color and detail elements to your page.

Rubber stamps can also be used in so many ways. You can stamp in one color or several different ones. Color them with chalks, pencils, markers, or paints. Use them to create background paper or for borders.

Stickers

Rubber Stamps

◆◆◆ themes ◆◆◆

What Kind of Themes Can I Choose From?

Albums are often organized around a single idea. Some of the most popular are . . .

Families	Friends
Babies	Kids
School Years	Weddings
Vacations	Sports
Holidays	Celebrations
Hobbies	Pets

Albums can also be centered around a single event such as a . . .

Wedding	Anniversary
Birthday	Reunion
Special Trip	Retirement
Graduation	New Baby
Easter	Halloween
Christmas	

Collect photos, postcards, and brochures to use in a theme album such as "My Trip to The Mission of San Juan Capistrano."

Other Ideas

Sometimes your photos may be placed in two different albums. For example, you may have pictures from Christmas in your family album along with all of the photos from one year, but you may also have an album that is a collection of all of your family Christmases through the years.

You may have an album that you develop over many years like a School Days album. Each year you add the important photos and memorabilia for one school year. By his or her senior year, you have the perfect gift to give the graduate.

You may want to make a Heritage album for each of your children. It is easy to make duplicates of photos so each child has his or her own personal family history.

You may want to make Memory Gifts for special people and occasions. They can be full-size albums, mini-albums, or even personalized cards that include photos. A scrapbook calendar also makes a great keepsake gift.

◆◆◆ reprints ◆◆◆

What is the Best Way to Make Copies of My Photos?

You have several choices, but NEVER cut an original photo that you cannot duplicate with a negative or that you do not have another copy of. When you have your film processed today, you can always get a second set of pictures; however, older photos may be one-of-a-kind. Be sure to get a reprint of the original or have it copied.

Here you can see the differences in some of the ways you can have a photo duplicated.

You may want a black and white copy to use for photo tinting.

A color photo copy or color reprint is best if you want a close duplication of the original photo. A color photo copy is usually printed on regular paper and does not provide as good a quality as a color reprint, which is printed on photo-quality paper.

A sepia tone reprint will be in brown tones for a vintage look.

#1 The Original

#2 Black & White Copy

#3 Color Photo Copy

#4 Sepia Tone Reprint

#5 Color Reprint

◆◆◆ cropping ◆◆◆

What is the Best Way to Crop My Photos?

Cropping a photo means to cut away the unimportant background that may be distracting. It puts the focus on a subject and can make a good photo great. When do you crop? When necessary to improve the photo or to creatively enhance it. Crop sparingly. Backgrounds often show details that are important to the time and place the photo was taken.

Needs cropping

Cropped too much

Cropped just right

Cutting Shapes

See how different the same photo can look when it is cropped in a variety of ways.

Original Photo

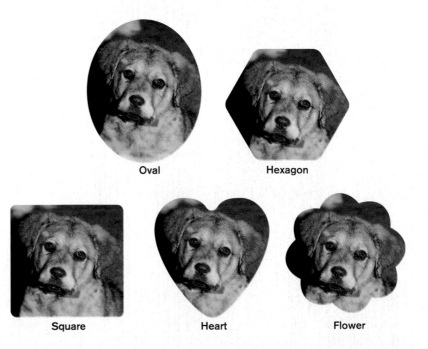

Oval

Hexagon

Square

Heart

Flower

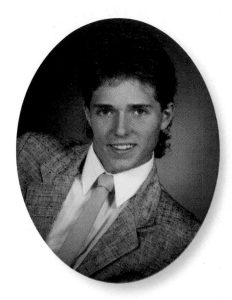

Formal photos look best when cut into ovals, circles, rectangles, or squares.

Save fun shapes for more informal photos. Use templates to complement pages with special themes. An unusual shape will highlight a photo, drawing attention to it.

Bumping a photo is cutting around only part of a person or object.

Silhouetting a photo is cutting around a person or object, which will make it stand out on the page. Choose a subject that has simple lines and don't cut too close to the object.

◆◆◆ matting ◆◆◆

What is the Best Way to Mat My Photos?

The easiest way is probably the best way. It's as Easy as 1 2 3.

Instructions

1 Glue your photo on the matting paper, allowing enough room for whatever width of border you want.

2 Draw a light pencil line around photo to indicate the outside edge of the mat.

3 Cut along lines with straight-edge or decorative-edge scissors.

Of course, there are a number of other options. Using a trimmer is a fast way to cut straight edges, and it will give you a clean crisp cut. A rotary cutter has interchangeable blades for cutting both straight and decorative edges. After you've matted a few photos, you may not feel you need to draw guidelines for cutting, which will speed up the process.

Crop photo

Mat photo on white paper

Mat photo on red paper

Create a Multiple Mat

Mat on light blue, then white, then dark blue paper. Glue blue photo corners on photo. Use white opaque marker to make small dots on dark blue mat and photo corners. Press three heart stickers on mat. Press rag doll sticker on mat.

◆◆◆ matting ◆◆◆

How Can I Cut a Decorative Edged Mat So the Corners Are the Same?

1 Cut strips of card stock to use as templates. Cut one long edge of each strip with a different decorative paper edger. Label each strip so you know which scissors you used. Punch a hole in the end of each strip and place them on a key ring.

2 Select which template you want to use. Position it on the edge of your photo so the pattern is the same at each corner point of photo. Hold securely in place and use as a cutting guide. If it feels awkward to hold the template, trace the design on the mat lightly with a pencil.

Still in Love
By Amy Gustafson for Hot Off The Press

Look at how creative matting can be! Two sides of the vellum mat are trimmed with Scallop paper edgers. The red mat is trimmed with the same edgers on the opposite sides. Two sides on the red mat are left extra wide for journaling. The heart is cut out with the same scissors, and a white gel pen is used to outline the edges. The final touch is placing the matted photo on an angle. It's a simple but dynamic page.

Which Scissors to Use?
To determine which decorative paper edger to use, consider the theme of your page. A pretty or romantic page calls for a multi-curved edge. A wavy edge is good for a beach page. You can also look at your photos and mimic the most dominant lines or shapes.

♦♦♦ layouts ♦♦♦

What Makes a Good Page Layout?

A layout is the arrangement of photos, lettering, shapes, and journaling on a page. A good layout accomplishes its purpose, which is to tell a story with photos, designs, and words. Organize your page so the viewer's eye travels through the page easily. The upper left corner is usually looked at first and eyes naturally go from left to right. A good layout includes the following things:

A Focal Point

A page needs a main center of interest that the eye is drawn to first. You can draw attention to something in different ways. You may enlarge a photo, place it in the center of the page, make it larger than all of the others, or mat it in a special way with the brightest colors on the page.

Balance

Items on the page have "weight" depending on their size, color, and complexity. Items that have more weight are larger, brighter in color, and are more complex. They draw attention to themselves.

The page should have balance from left to right and from top to bottom. That doesn't mean pages must be symmetrical, the same on the left as on the right. Asymmetrical pages can be balanced, too. Two examples of creating balance are offsetting one large photo with two small ones or by using one brightly colored mat to offset two plainer ones. If you have two pages side by side, they should also be balanced with each other.

Experiment by moving the elements of your page around before gluing them down. Your eye will be your guide. Remember that journaling will also play a part in how well your page is balanced.

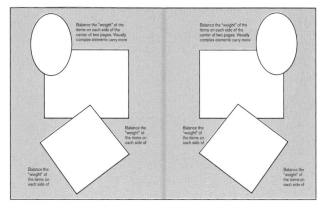

Symmetrical

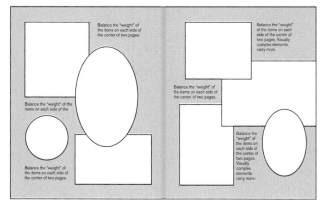

Asymmetrical

Color

The use of color throughout your page also affects the balance. Use papers that enhance the colors in your photos. Choose attractive color combinations that work well together. Use contrasting colors to separate the different elements on your page. Solid colors should be used to separate patterned papers.

Variation

Use different photo sizes and shapes to add interest to your pages. The largest photo will get the most attention. Combine squares and rectangles with circles and ovals. Use photos that have been "bumped" or "silhouetted" for variation.

Connections

Use different ways to connect the elements on the page to guide your eye as it travels from one to the next. Overlap photos and shapes. Don't forget that journaling can connect one photo to another, too.

Bugs Have Rights
By Carol Snyder for EK Success

This is a good example of a well-balanced asymmetrical layout. The horizontal tree branch at the top of the page balances with the horizontal grass at the bottom of the page. The shorter photo on the left allows room for the photo hanging from the branch. The space above the taller photo is the perfect place for a title.

Notice the repetition of color and its placement throughout the page. Red, yellow, blue, and green are evenly distributed. The bugs tie the page together.

◆◆◆ journaling ◆◆◆

Why is Journaling Important to Include on My Pages?

Telling the story behind the photos in your albums is one of the most important things you can do to pass down your family history for future generations. The more information you include, the more valuable each page in your album becomes.

The Basic Facts

Answer the questions Who? What? When? Where? Why? and How? It can be as simple as just labeling the photos.

Added Details

Give additional information behind the basic facts. You may want to write it in bulleted form or be more creative and wrap it around the photos as shown here.

When writing a narrative, choose from one of the following point of views in which you will tell the story.

First Person

Tell the story from a personal point of view. Use the word "I." It can be a story that you are telling from your own personal experience, or you can assume the persona of someone else. For example, you may tell a story as if you were your grandmother speaking.

Second Person

Tell the story as if you were talking to someone else. Use the word "you." This is especially good to use if you are creating an album for someone special and you are talking to them.

Third Person

Tell the story as if it happened to someone else. Use the words "he," "she," and "it." This is more like reporting what happened, and it is less personal.

Storytelling

Tell the story behind the photos in narrative form, including descriptive details. You can include longer journaling by creating a pocket by gluing two papers together along three sides as shown here. In this case, an extra photo was even included with the journaling page, which was inserted into the pocket.

◆ ◆ ◆ journaling ◆

Journaling Template

Journaling Template

There are many creative ways to add journaling to your pages. Printing or writing with your own hand certainly makes your pages more personal. If you don't like the look of your penmanship, you can always use the computer, which offers many different type styles to fit in with the themes of your pages. Some of the fonts even look like handwriting.

Journaling templates offer you a guide for journaling within creative shapes. They have lines that you can pencil in and erase when your journaling is done.

What do you do when you don't have enough room to journal on your pages? Make more room with pockets and envelopes! You can also create pull-tabs. You will find more journaling ideas throughout this book.

A big pocket on the page is the perfect place to store journaling, report cards, ribbons, and other school mementos.

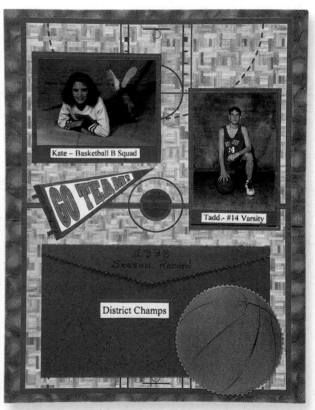

Make an envelope that coordinates with the rest of the page to hold journaling, programs, records, etc.

◆◆◆ protecting ◆◆◆

How Can I Preserve My Photos?

It is important to use archival-quality materials to preserve photographs. You have probably noticed that many of your old pictures have lost their color or clarity over the years. Photographs go through a chemical process in development, which subjects them to natural ongoing deterioration. With careful handling, photos can last for hundreds of years. Be aware of the dangers and how best to protect your photos from harm.

Photo Dangers

Acidity (low pH)

PVC (polyvinylchloride, which breaks down to hydrochloric acid)

Humidity

"Magnet" Albums

Dust and Dirt

Sunlight

Ball-Point and Felt-Tip Pens

Fingerprints

Extreme Temperatures

Photos can deteriorate over time.

What Can I Do With Damaged Photos?

Check with your local photography store about having photos restored. You can also use the Kodak Picturemaker to restore photos and adjust colors, but copyrighted photography cannot be duplicated.

The Restored Photo

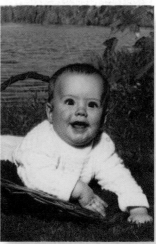

The Damaged Original

Where Can I Find Inspiration for My Scrapbook Pages?

Don't limit yourself to scrapbook idea books and magazines – look at the world around you! Design and layout ideas are always at your fingertips if you take time to notice. The following list of ideas should get you started. Add your own ideas as you sharpen your powers of observation.

Reprinted with permission from the September/October 2000 issue of Memory Makers magazine.

Postcards.

All those "wish you were here" postcards might cause you to take a trip of your own - to your scrapbook table, with cards in hand as inspiration. This page was inspired by a postcard featuring a collage of photographs.

Postage Stamps.

Copy the ruffled edge of a postage stamp around the edge of a page and adapt old-fashioned stamp elements to frame a portrait.

Fabric.

Patterns from clothing, curtains, tablecloths, and other fabrics might be just the style needed for a page border or background idea.

Dishes.

Mimic the look and pattern of a decorative plate or bowl.

Packaging.

Adapt the packaging from a child's favorite snack for a scrapbook page or use the packaging of everyday products from around your home.

Paper Towels.

Copy a paper towel's quilted effect using embossing paper or adapt the printed pattern to create guidelines for your own page.

Television.

Use elements from a favorite television show as inspiration for a fun scrapbook page.

Gift Wrap.

Wrapping paper and gift bags can offer unique patterns and color combinations to page layouts.

License Plates.

Document a vacation to a certain state or country by creating a page based on that location's license plate.

Junk Mail.

Get layout ideas from pamphlets, fliers, coupons, and other things you get in the mail.

Fine Art.

Your layouts will truly become works of art when elements from the style of famous artists are incorporated on your pages.

♦♦♦ styles ♦♦♦

Are There Different Scrapbooking Styles?

According to scrapbooking expert Stacy Julian, style is how you choose to use certain elements on your page. While design principles such as color, shape, and line can help you position your page elements well, it's the specific appearance of those elements that helps determine style. Because the page style is a reflection of the scrapbooker's unique tastes and personality, there's no wrong or right style. It's simply a matter of expressing yourself as you emphasize the photos on your page.

Photographer Deidre Haines of Garland, Texas, took the vintage-style photos used on the pages presented here. The pictures were given to five top scrapbookers to use on pages that illustrate different page styles.

While everyone's style is unique, most pages fit into one of five general categories identified by Stacy Julian and Kim McCrary, a creative editor for Creating Keepsakes magazine.

1 Classic

This style tends to use darker, solid colors in shades such as navy, burgundy, and forest green, along with white, off-white, and black. The design is generally both simple and 'timeless." Embossing and straight lines lend an elegant look that's crisp and clean. Embellishments are subtle.

2 Playful Charm

This style incorporates complementary colors in muted or bright tones. You'll find coordinating patterns, checks, dots, stripes, and playful accents such as paper dolls, paper piecing, and cute lettering.

◆◆◆ styles ◆◆◆

3 Naturalist

This style gets "back to nature" with earth tones, speckled paper, and monochromatic color schemes, such as several shades of green. Textures such as mulberry and jute are common, as are torn edges.

4 Contemporary

This style 'pulls out the stops" with bold patterns and accents. The look is modern and may include strong accents such as prominent artwork, geometric shapes, and metallic papers.

5 Romantic

This style includes floral patterns, lace, vellum, doilies, and softer colors. Text is often presented in script or a feminine-looking font.

1 Designed by Kim McCrary
2 Designed by Brenda Birrell and Liza Belmont
3 Designed by Rebecca Sower
4 Designed by Christine Peterson
5 Designed by Jennifer McLaughlin

◆◆◆ light table ◆◆◆

How Can I Use a Light Table?

A light table is used when you need a light source for seeing through a photo or paper. It is usually used when tracing something. You can place what you want to trace on a window and use the sun as your light source, but it is clumsy and the sun does not provide twenty-four hours of light.

You will use a light table most often for tracing alphabets and designs. Another use is when using a template to crop a photo. The advantage of using the light table is that you can see through the photo and can position the template just the way you want it on the back of the photo. By marking the back, you can avoid the danger of possibly damaging the front of the photo. Another use for a light table is when you are embossing.

Tracing a letter or design. Place the alphabet right side up on the table. Place paper over the letters you want to use. You can trace the letters with a pencil first and then use a marker — or use the marker to do the initial tracing.

Cropping a photo using a template. Place the photo face down on the table. Position the template over the photo and trace around it with a photo-safe marker.

Embossing a design. Tape stencil on paper. Trace design using a stylus.

◆◆◆ die cutting ◆◆◆

How Can I Use Die Cuts On My Pages?

Die cuts can be used for titles, journaling, and for adding interesting shapes to your page to fit in with a specific theme or style.

Multiple shapes, letters, and numbers can be cut quickly using a die-cutting system. Your local scrapbooking or craft store will probably have one available for you to use if you don't want to purchase your own machine. Precut die cuts are also available packaged by themes or colors.

Katie and Prince
By Julie Stephani for Krause Publications

The lettering die cuts used on this page were cut using two different colors. Putting them slightly offset from each other gives a shadowed or dimensional effect. Usually the darker color would be underneath for shadow, but for this page, the lighter yellow made a better contrast against the plaid background. The letters are placed at different angles for added interest. Journaling was done on the computer in order to tell more details in a small space.

Prince was a very special member of the family. We bought him from a family who raised collies for dog shows. We chose Prince because he had quite a bit of black hair which was more defining. They discounted the price because he had one ear that did not stand up straight. We didn't care if it did.

Prince was always a gentle dog but was also protective of our place. He tangled with several porcupine and skunk over the years.

He died the fall of 1990 before we moved to Illinois. We buried him south of the house next to Casper, our white cat.

The Die Cutting Process
Place the die with blade/sponge right side up on the tray. Place the paper on top of the die. Several sheets of paper can be cut at one time. Turn the handle to run the die through the machine. Remove die cuts and paper.

1 Lay paper over die.

2 Turn the handle.

3 Remove die cuts.

Bouncin' Round

By Carol Snyder for EK Success

Punch circles out of beige background paper so they look like they are bouncing down the sides of the page. Punch some partial circles on the edges of the paper. Glue an orange strip of paper on back of each side of paper so orange shows through. Draw lines on each basketball with black marker. Draw dash lines to show the bouncing path of the balls.

Punch rectangles in bottom of page — one for each letter of the name. Punch four stars to right of rectangles. Write name in rectangles and the word "star" in stars. Cut a large purple half-circle and glue towards top of page.

Cut photos into several sizes of circles. Mat on orange paper to match basketballs. Glue on page so they get larger as they go down the page.

Write title on yellow paper, leaving space to place basketball stickers in place of O's. Add dash bounce lines. Add journaling.

How Can I Use Circles Creatively?

A circle is such a simple shape, but just look at what you can do with them. Use them to mat photos or for design elements on the page.

Mouse Magic
By Julie McGuffee

Use circle cutter to crop photos into one large circle for head and two smaller circles for ears. Adjust cutter to make black mats larger, leaving borders of ½" for head and ¼" for ears. Cut three stars from yellow paper using a star die. Cut letters from black and white paper using a die. Glue white letters on black letters, slightly to one side. Cut gloved hands freehand from white paper. Position pieces on paper and glue in place.

Pumpkins All Around
Design by Fiskars

Crop two photos and trim corners with Rounder corner edgers. Mat on yellow paper and trim with Scallop paper edgers. Cut third photo into a circle, using the circle cutter. Cut a 4" circle from orange paper. Cut a 3" circle out of the center of it. Position photos and circles on page.

For pumpkin, cut a 3" circle from orange card stock. Position cutter ½" from one side of circle. Start in middle and turn cutter to left and cut to end of circle. Repeat on opposite side. Run three pieces through crimper. For leaves, fold green card stock and cut on the fold with Wide Seagull paper edgers. For hay bale, cut rectangle with Wide Deckle paper edger and run through crimper. Position pieces on leaf background paper and glue in place.

◆ ◆◆ ◆ ovals ◆◆◆ ◆

How Can I Use Ovals Creatively?

An oval is one of the most attractive and often used shapes for cropping photos. Ovals can also be used as paper accents and for journaling guides.

Baby Collage
By Cj Wilson for Accu-Cut

This composite of baby pictures is created using a Multiple Ovals Picture Frame die and the die-cutting system. Glue pink paper on white card stock for strength, then cut the ovals using the die. Use a stylus to trace photo openings onto photos. Trim photos a scant ¼" outside trace lines. Position photos in openings and glue in place. Cut a bow and pieces from Scherenschnitte to embellish page. Glue in place.

◆◆◆ ovals ◆◆◆

Add Dimension

Use a crimper to create textured paper by running it through two metal barrels that leave imprints. A variety of patterns can be made by changing angles and running paper through the crimper more than once.

From this . . .

. . . to this!

Chip Lips
Design by Fiskars

Look at the difference when dimensional ovals and journaling are added to the page! Cut photos into oval shapes and mat on yellow paper with a very thin border. Then mat on green rectangles that have the corners trimmed with Blossom corner edgers. What really makes this page special are the yellow ovals that are run though the crimper to give them the look of potato chips! They are the perfect addition to capture the fun!

Crimper

◆ ◆ ◆ shapes ◆ ◆ ◆

What Can I Do With a Paper Shaper?

This tool is great for cutting free-form shapes as well as using with a template guide. The flexible blade rotates around curves. With a little practice, you'll be cutting shapes as quickly as you can draw them.

The Big Splash
By Barb Lashua for Fiskars

The paper shaper makes a big splash on this page! It's the perfect shape to accent the photos of baby cooling off in the pool. Keep enough paper in the center open for journaling. Overlap the shapes and photos to tie the page together.

Paper Shaper

◆◆◆ lace ◆◆◆

How Can I Create Lace Using Paper?

The lacy matting on this lovely bridal photo was created with just one decorative scissors. Each row of lace is made by cutting a very thin strip of paper. The rows are then glued in place in graduating lengths.

Maria 1999
Design by Fiskars

Mat photo on white card stock, leaving a very thin border. To make lace, draw a straight line with a ruler along one length of white card stock. Using the Seagull paper edgers, cut along the edge of the line so the tip of the pattern touches the line. Cut a parallel cut as thin as possible. The thinner the strip, the more delicate the lace will appear.

Cut a strip to fit across the top of photo and glue in place. Place the next strip above the first so the arches are staggered. Glue in place. Each row will have two fewer arches, so the lace will come to a point. Repeat the same process to create lace at the bottom of the photo.

Embellish corners using white teardrop punches and a small length of lace paper.

◆◆◆ puzzles ◆◆◆

How Can I Create a Puzzle-Piece Look?

It's easy because most of the work is done for you if you use a puzzle template or a puzzle die and the die-cutting system. It's just a question of cutting out the puzzle shapes from photos and/or paper that will fit together on your page.

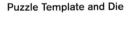

Puzzle Template and Die

Family Tree
By Cj Wilson for Accu-Cut

This page looks like an exploded puzzle because the pieces have space between them. Mat tan background paper on olive green paper. Use a die to cut out two branches with leaves, two light tan and two dark green. Glue on the page, offsetting the pieces so the green looks like a shadow.

Use the photo template to trace puzzle shapes on the back of photos Cut out and glue on the page, weaving the branches and photos around each other. Trace the journaling puzzle piece and cut out of olive green paper, having the paper folded at the top. Print journaling on the inside and "Family Tree" on the top. Glue on the page. Use a brown chisel marker to draw the straight lines around each corner.

Kickers

By Cj Wilson for Accu-Cut

Use a 12" x 12" cranberry red background paper for this page. Center an 11" x 11¼" dark blue paper and glue on the background. Glue an 8" x 10" light blue paper ¾" from bottom of page. Cut letters from red and light blue papers, using a lettering die. Glue the blue on the red and then on the top of the page, staggering the letters. Use a blue marker to write the letters on the die cuts.

This puzzle page has all of the pieces fitting closely together. Use the template to trace the puzzle piece shapes on the back of the photos, using the two left corners and then every other piece. Cut out and glue them on the light blue paper. Use a red marker to draw stitch lines around the puzzle pieces between the photos. Use a blue pen to add the journaling and hearts.

Norway

By Cj Wilson for Accu-Cut

This is a variation of a similar page on page 47. Mat photo on black and then blue paper, leaving 1/8" borders. Create a paper-pieced scene using die-cut shapes. Arrange pieces on white background paper and glue in this order: photo, turquoise water, tan sand, brown tree trunk (crimped), green grass and tree top, and yellow sun. Cut red and white letters for title. Glue white letters over red ones. Glue letters on page.

Arizona
By Barb Lashua for Fiskars

You only need a few elements to create a scene. Cut three papers along one edge with Long Deckle paper edgers. Layer them along the bottom of page, inserting one photo between two of them. Use the computer to print the journaling and trim with Aztec paper edgers. Mat on brown paper and cut in same way. Use same scissors to cut two similar shapes from tan and brown paper. Use Wide Seagull paper edgers to cut the rust pot. Cut a partial sun with Long Deckle paper edgers. Cut a cactus shape. Crop photos and round corners using a Round corner edgers. Position pieces on page and glue in place.

The Mountains
Designed by Fiskars

Use your photos to choose the colors for the mountain background. Cut papers into mountain peaks and one green paper into treetops with Large Deckle paper edgers. Arrange on blue background paper and glue in place, leaving tree tops loose for inserting photo.

Mat photos on lavender paper and trim with Pinking paper edgers. Glue photos on page, tucking bottom photo underneath treetops.

◆◆◆ mosaics ◆◆◆

How Can I Make A Photo Mosaic?

The concept is basic: cut your photos into squares using a grid and arrange them as you like. This arrangement of photo tiles can be simple, involving a few photos, or can be a complex overlapping of numerous photos.

Dad in His Workshop
By Lenae Gerig for Hot Off the Press

The mosaic photo mats duplicate the border on the patterned paper. White and deep country red ⅜" squares are glued along the edges of black mats. Four squares glued on the corners of the journaling box add the final touch.

Colorado Trip

By Michele Gerbrandt for Memory Makers

This page is more complex, combining three photos that are cut into 1"squares and two photos left uncut. The borders are made up of ⅛", ¼", and ½ " squares that have been punched out of photos. All of the elements are glued on the dark turquoise background paper.

Basic Photo Mosaic

1. Select photos and arrange on your page.

2. Using a photo-safe pencil and ruler, draw a grid of squares on back of each photo. Label individual squares on back of photos. See illustration. For example: 1a, 1b, 1c, etc. on first photo; 2a, 2b, 2c, etc. on second photo.

3. Cut photos into squares and put each photo in an envelope or plastic bag to keep separated.

4. Arrange squares as desired. Glue squares on page.

1A	1B	1C	1D
1E	1F	1G	1H
1I	1J	1K	1L
1M	1N	1O	1P
1Q	1R	1S	1T
1U	1V	1W	1X

On the back of the photo, number each square before cutting.

◆◆◆ braiding ◆◆◆

How Can I Make a Braided Border?

Cut two or three thin strips of paper using a decorative paper edger. Wrap the strips around each other to make either a double or triple braid.

The Fiskars River
Designed by Fiskars

Cut mats just slightly larger than the photo in two different colors. Using Wave paper edgers, cut thin slits in the bottom two corners. Arrange mats and photo on page at different angles. Glue down, fanning cuts in photo.

Make paper braids as explained on this page. Cut three braids to fit diagonally across top right corner. Lay one strip over bottom of mat and write journaling on it. Cut one edge of three strips of paper in same coordinating colors and layer them across bottom of page.

Paper Braiding
Using the Wide Wave paper edgers, cut two or three identical strips ¼" wide or less in coordinating colors. *Note: Place papers together and cut them at the same time to make identical strips and save time.* Weave strips around each other, going the opposite directions if using two strips and going the same direction if using three strips.

Paper strips can be wrapped around each other in several different ways.

♦♦♦ paper chains ♦♦♦

How Can I Make a Paper-Chain Border?

Cut paper along a fold to create the look of beading lace. Insert a small paper-chain through the holes of a larger one.

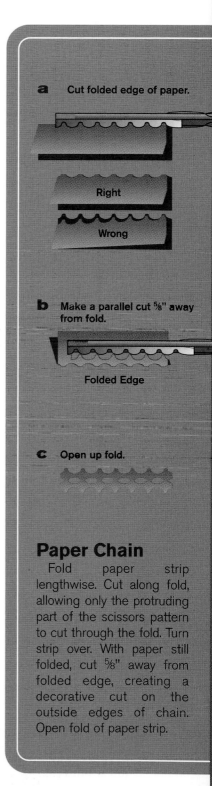

a Cut folded edge of paper.

Right

Wrong

b Make a parallel cut ⅝" away from fold.

Folded Edge

c Open up fold.

Paper Chain

Fold paper strip lengthwise. Cut along fold, allowing only the protruding part of the scissors pattern to cut through the fold. Turn strip over. With paper still folded, cut ⅝" away from folded edge, creating a decorative cut on the outside edges of chain. Open fold of paper strip.

Fiskars First Logo
Designed by Fiskars

Cut first two mats with Seagull paper edgers. Cut third mat with Long Seagull paper edgers. Punch ⅛" holes in third mat. Cut a rectangle for journaling box. Trim corners with Regal corner edgers. Glue corner cuts on page in a two matching designs.

Cut two paper chains as explained on this page, smaller one with Long Seagull and larger one with Wide Seagull paper edgers.

How Can I Include Paper Dolls on My Pages?

One of the most fun design elements to add to your pages is paper dolls. You can buy paper dolls in packages that include all of the pieces to dress them in special outfits, or use die cuts and templates to customize them to coordinate with the photos or theme of your pages.

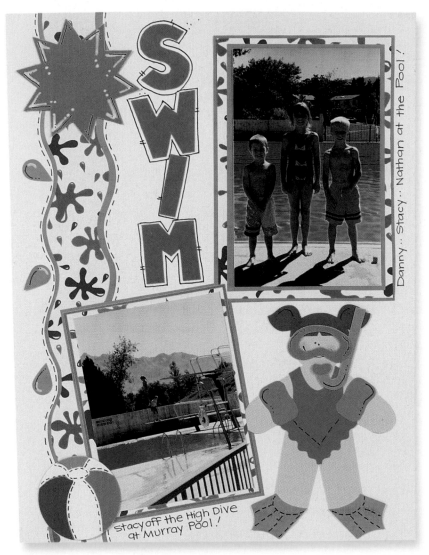

Danny · · Stacy · · Nathan at the Pool !

Stacy off the High Dive at Murray Pool !

Swim

By Carol Snyder for EK Success

Cut 2" off left side of white background paper using a wave template. Glue a 2" strip of "splash" patterned paper along left side. Glue white paper back on over splash paper, leaving 1" of splash paper showing. Trim left side of white paper so page measures 8½" wide.

Use a template to trace around letters and cutout. Mat photos on patterned paper, then plain paper. Glue paper doll together. Arrange pieces on page, including sun and beach ball die cuts. Glue in place.

◆◆◆ paper dolls ◆◆◆

S.S. Norway
By Cj Wilson for Accu-Cut

Crop photos into various sizes of ovals. Create a paper-pieced scene using die-cut shapes. Arrange pieces on black background paper and glue in this order: photos, turquoise water, tan sand, brown tree trunk, green grass and tree top, and yellow sun. Cut a white banner for title. Write the letters or use stickers for the title.

Cut a blue and a white ship. Cut smokestacks and bottom off of white ship. Glue white ship on blue ship. Cut a red strip and glue on base of white piece. Glue ship on page.

Cut out paper doll. Cut at joints to position in an animated pose. Dress appropriately and add detail lines with black marker.

Walking the Dog
By Jill Rinner for Accu-Cut

Make a paper doll and puppy that can go on any page you choose. Cut out doll, clothes, hair, dog, and leash. Glue pieces together. Punch a small circle for the dog tag and a heart for his nose. Draw eyes and mouths with black marker.

◆◆◆ paper dolls ◆◆◆

Ready-Set-Grow!

By Carol Snyder for EK Success

Include a growth chart in your scrapbook to record vital statistics for the growing years. Trace letters and numbers using a template. Cut 2" wide strips for ruler – one tan and one brown. Use a rectangle punch to cut out the "inch" marks from tan paper. Glue tan paper on brown paper. Cut out numbers and glue on ruler. For words, trace letter on colored paper, overlapping letters slightly. Cut around each word, leaving a ⅛" border. Add details with marker. Glue on page.

Mat a special photo. Dress your paper doll in whatever outfit you think is appropriate. Glue both on the page. Print the information you want to record.

◆◆◆ kids ◆◆◆

How Can I Involve My Kids in Scrapbooking?

Scrapbooking is perfect for kids. They love creating pages all about themselves, their friends and family, their pets, and all of the fun things they like to do. Set out some supplies that focus on their interests and give them a few tools to work with. Then stand back! Don't get in the way when the creative sparks begin to fly!

Kiddsors Decorative Paper Edgers

Kid's Pages

By Barb Lashua for Fiskars

What could be more perfect for kids' school pages than background papers that look like a chalkboard and theme paper. Show them how to mat their photos. Give them stickers, punch-outs, pens, and Kidssors – decorative paper edgers that are just their size – and just watch what they will come up with.

Mom & Me

By Julie Stephani for Krause Publications

Kids love to scrapbook, too! Let them get involved in creating pages especially for them. If you are working together, both of you can take on different tasks. Let the child pick out the pictures. You can do the matting that takes more precise cutting, but let the child punch out the shapes. On this page there are squares, hearts, dots, and paw prints. You may want to help position the pieces exactly on the page, but let the child help apply the glue. In this way you have created a "tag team," and you will feel good about creating something memorable together.

How Can I Plan Ahead for Framed Photos?

There are some photos that you will want to keep in a frame for a period of time before putting them in your albums. School pictures are just one example. First, I created the page, including a matting for the photo. Then I placed the matted photo in a frame. I inserted the page in a protective sleeve and put it in the back of my album. When my granddaughter's new class picture arrives next year, I will remove this one from the frame and place it on its page that has already been completed.

The final page

The prepared page

The framed photo

Krista Michelle

By Julie Stephani for Krause Publications

This page was a fun one to do because I had some good elements to work with in the photo. I picked papers that had denim and overall patterns and used gold as an accent to match the patch on the bib overalls. Then it was just a question of making multiple mats using contrasting colors next to each other. Each large photo corner was made by matting a large triangle twice. A few stitching lines were the final detail.

What Are Some Creative Ways for Kids to Use Mini Albums?

The sky's the limit! Albums are great for displaying photos of friends, their favorite hobbies, sports, events, or whatever they want. There are lots of supplies that are especially great for kids, like bright papers, stickers, punch-outs, stamps, and decorative edged scissors.

Inside page

6" x 9" Album

My School Friends

By Vivian Grothe

For album cover, cut a 4" x 7" piece of white paper. Mat with blue, then yellow, then blue paper, varying the width of the borders. Decorate with stickers and letters. Use markers to add squiggly lines and dots. Matted piece can be laminated for durability. Glue matted piece on front cover.

For page, cut a solid color and a patterned paper to fit album page. Tear patterned paper in two strips – one large for photo, one smaller for name. Add stickers and letters. Each page in the album can be done this way, changing the colors and patterns of paper.

2¾" x 3" Album

Best Buds Album

By Julie Stephani for Krause Publications

For cover, cut a 1" x 2" piece of white paper. Mat with green paper, cut with Mini Scallop paper edgers. Glue on top of cover. Decorate with a flower sticker and letters.

For Kris page, mat photo on green, then white paper, leaving enough room at bottom of writing name. Decorate with stickers. Cut 1¾" x 2½" piece of white paper for journaling. Mat on yellow paper. Write journaling. Use green photo corners to attach to page.

For Kate page, mat and decorate photo in same way. For envelope, cut a 2" x 3¼" rectangle. Cut one end in a point. Fold pointed end down ¾" from end for flap. Fold again so other end is up against fold of flap. Note: See page 96 for envelope pattern.

◆ ◆ ◆ punch-outs ◆ ◆ ◆

How Can I Use Punch-Outs on My Pages?

Use punch-outs for titles, matting accents, or to create a scene! They are already matted with a white edging that will make them "pop" off the page. Move them around on the page until you find the perfect position. What could be easier!

Happy Birthday Zakk
By Lenae Gerig for Hot Off the Press

Animal punch-outs add a whimsical touch to a birthday page. Use creative paper piecing to create a scene. Use cloud paper for the background and cut a hill from grass paper. Cut a path from cobblestone paper and mat it on black paper, cutting a very scant border. Cut the sign from barn-wood paper. Glue the scene together, inserting matted photos behind the hill. Have fun positioning the punch-outs before gluing them in place.

punch-outs

Katrina

By Juile Stephani for Krause Publications

Mat a single photo on a page and create a larger frame in order to include comical animal punch-outs on the matting. These characters look like they are peeking out around the frame! Add foam adhesive dots or strips behind each punch-out to add dimension to the page.

Use white paper and two additional colors for the die-cut letters. The white "shadow" behind the colored letters really makes them "pop" off the page. It also matches the white matting around the punch-outs.

How Can I Use Punches to Make Decorative Borders?

Create a border by arranging punched shapes in a strip down one side, several sides, or all four sides of a page. Begin with a strip of paper that looks like a ribbon with "v" cut ends, or arrange punched shapes in a line so they overlap each other. Use these examples to get you started but custom-make your own borders to coordinate with your unique themes and style.

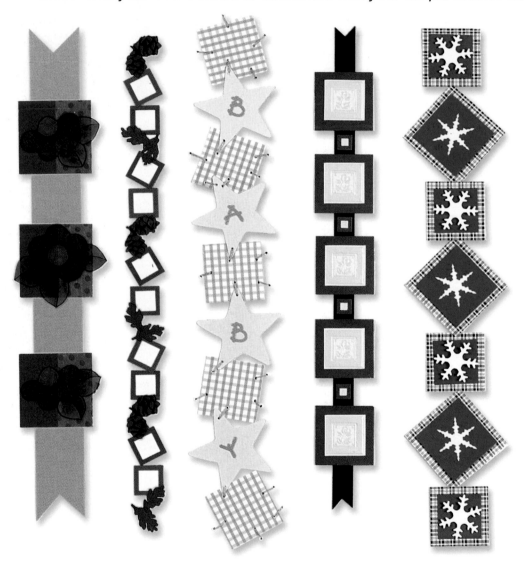

Border Techniques with Punches
By Kristy Banks for Creating Keepsakes

See photo to determine shapes and position. Punched shapes are layered and overlapped in a line to create borders but could also be used for accents anywhere on the page. Vary colors to match the colors in the photos. Use the punches upside down to make it easier for positioning them.

How Can I Use Punch Shapes Creatively on My Pages?

Punch shapes can be used to create all kinds of shapes and objects by combining several of them together. One of the secrets is finding the right shapes − and the other is selecting the right papers.

Mother's Day
By Shauna Berglund Emmel for Hot Off the Press

This is a great example of making all of the right choices. The flowers and leaves are simple but very effective with the perfect choice of papers and very thin border around each one. It makes them "pop" off the page. What also helps is the dimensional foam tape behind each one!

Mats are cut with straight-edge scissors and also with the Deckle, Scallop, and Mini Scallop paper edgers. Journaling is done with cursive handwriting and a computer script font. The combination works well together.

◆ ◆ ◆ punches ◆ ◆ ◆

How Can I Use Punches With Patterned Paper?

These daisies are a perfect example of how to use punches to duplicate a design that is in a patterned paper.

In the Garden
By Shauna Berglund-Immel for Hot Off the Press

This page also shows that matching florals and patterned papers is easy and adds style to your scrapbook page. Two different patterned papers with soft hues of lavender coordinate well together. Cut 2½" off the bottom of the floral paper, using a template or decorative-edge scissors. Cut a 1" wide white strip and glue behind this wave edge. Trim the white paper, leaving a ¹⁄₁₆" border. Glue a 2½" wide strip of striped paper behind the wave edge so page measures 12" x 12".

For each daisy, begin with two leaves as the base. Punch 16 teardrop shapes for petals. Arrange eight teardrops in a circle for the first layer of petals. Use eight more for the second layer, placing each petal between two petals of the first layer.

Mat the photo and journaling boxes with white paper to set them off from the patterned background. Journal in white ink for the final perfect touch.

◆◆◆ punches ◆◆◆

How Can I Duplicate My Pages to Share with Others?

Sometimes we would like to share our scrapbook pages with others, but it would take too much time to duplicate the pages several times. You can make a color copy of the page, and the result is surprisingly good quality. You can also make a reprint of the page in the same way you would reprint a photograph, but you will have to adjust the size slightly to accommodate the standard photo sizes.

The original page

The 5" x 7" duplicated page used as a photo on a different page

Graduation
By Julie McGuffee for Kodak

This page was a little more time-consuming because of the tiny punched designs, so when grandparents asked for copies, Julie decided to make a reprint of the page using the Kodak Picturemaker. She reduced it to a smaller 5" x 7" size and liked the result so much that she decided to frame it and make another slightly different page. The second page was the one she decided to duplicate for both sets of grandparents.

◆ ◆ ◆ stickers ◆ ◆ ◆

How Can I Use Stickers When Matting Photos?

Stickers are great to use as decorative accents on your mats. Who said mats had to have straight edges? Cut the mat around the outline of the stickers to create a really unique frame around your photo.

Golf Champions
By Carol Snyder for EK Success

Mat the photo on white or a light color, leaving enough width to use for journaling. The grass along the bottom edge gives the photo an appropriate base. Place stickers around the second colored mat so they are arranged lengthwise. Cut around stickers, leaving an even border around each sticker.

This matted photo could be framed or placed on a page. You could also use stickers in the same way around a full page. The plastic sleeve will protect the protruding points.

How Can I Get Pages Done Quickly After a Vacation?

You'll have pages done within days following your vacation if you do what Julie McGuffee did. She used a digital camera, planned some clever journaling photos ahead of time, and used stickers for decorative details.

Memory cards from a digital camera can be developed immediately by taking it to a Kodak Picturemaker at your local store. Insert the card into the adapter, then view your pictures on the screen. Choose the ones you like best, edit as necessary, then print. That's exactly how the photos on these pages were printed. The day after Julie arrived home from her family vacation in Mexico, she was able to go right to work capturing her memories on her scrapbook pages.

Mexico
By Julie McGuffee for Kodak

Colorful stickers are used for "Mexico" and "2000" and carry the ocean theme throughout both pages. The dash lines connecting the feet also connect one page to the other by crossing over in the center of the spread. Note the clever journaling photo that took just a little extra planning while on the beach. "Cozumel" was printed in the sand, substituting a shell for the "O." For added extra interest her family's feet were included in the photo. The "pin" marks in the top corners of each picture are a nice detail that completes the pages.

◆ ◆ ◆ scherenschnitte ◆ ◆ ◆

How Can I Use Scherenschnitte on My Pages?

The intricately cut paper is perfect for scrapbooking pages. It's already cut so all you have to do is place it on your page. It can also be cut apart and different elements of the design can be used for corners, borders, or accents anywhere on the page.

Top left: Aunt Babe, Aunt Vi & Wilma (grandma)
Top right: Gertrude (grandma)
Bottom right: LuAnn (mom)

Babies
From the
Past

Babies from the Past
By Cj Wilson for Accu-Cut

Look at the variety of ways scherenschnitte can be used on a page to frame the photos. Full sheets can be cut apart to create frames and accents. Even the bow is a cut piece. It really enhances the photos to create a vintage page.

scherenschnitte

Senior Class

By Cj Wilson for Accu-Cut

Dark blue background paper was trimmed ½" on top and one side, then glued on center of gray paper. The photo, invitation, and small card were matted on red paper and trimmed to ¼" borders. All of the pieces were positioned on the page, and the scherenschnitte pieces were cut to fill in around the edges of the page. Then everything was glued in place.

◆ ◆ ◆ chalks ◆ ◆ ◆

How Can I Use Chalk on My Pages?

Chalk can be used to add color on any pages, but it works especially well when using scherenschnitte. The subtle shades and intricate cuts are a perfect combination. You may want to spray the chalk with a fixative to set it.

June

By Cj Wilson for Accu-Cut

Cut ½" from top and and one side of roses paper. Round corners using a decorative corner edgers. Glue on black card stock. Round corners of card stock.

Cut black and white letters using a lettering die and the die-cutting system. Glue black letters over white ones, slightly to one side.

Color the scherenschnitte with chalk before gluing it on the 8½" x 11½" black paper. Round the corners of black paper. Cut the photo in an oval to fit inside opening. Glue photo in opening. Position this piece along with letters and bird design on roses background. Glue in place.

◆◆◆ chalks ◆◆◆

Falling Leaves
By Cj Wilson for Accu-Cut

Cut tan, green, and red card stock using a basket die and the die-cutting system. Use the tan basket as the base. Cut off top green rim and glue on basket. Cut off red band and glue on basket. Cut gold, red, and orange card stock using a leaf die. Apply chalk to each leaf, varying the colors of chalk. Cut red and green card stock using an apple die.

Chalk the stem brown and the leaf green. Cut light brown cardstock using a tree die. Draw grain marks along branches and trunk with black marker. Cut gold cardstock using the letters die. Chalk with red and orange. Position pieces on background. Trim tree branches even with edge of page.

Mat photos with fall colored mats. Position pieces on page. Glue in place.

Melodie & Aaron
By Cj Wilson for Accu-Cut

A clever way to coordinate two pages is to use a scherenschnitte design from the first page for a stencil on the following page. Print the poem on the computer before stenciling the design. Add two additional hearts to the second page, using dimensional foam dots to raise them up and give the page dimension.

How Can I Use Doodles on My Pages?

Use your creative doodles to make background designs for your album pages. Start with a piece of white card stock and try some of the following simple doodles using specialty markers. Pick your favorites and try a whole page of doodles!

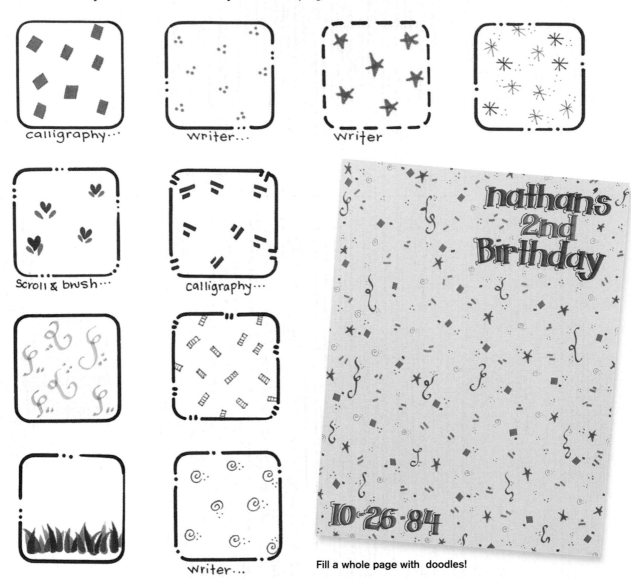

calligraphy…

writer…

writer

scroll & brush…

calligraphy…

writer…

Fill a whole page with doodles!

Tip

Save your original doodle page and make color copies to use for patterned paper. Enlarge or reduce the copy to get variations. See the enlarged doodle pattern on the next page.

Happy Birthday Stacy
By Carol Snyder for EK Success

This was a special page for Stacy who turned 20 in the year 2000. The picture is matted on white card stock, leaving a ½" border. The large end of a calligraphy marker easily created a checkerboard design on the corners, leaving room for journaling in between. Two solid colored mats separate the photo from the fun doodle background paper.

◆◆◆ colored pencils ◆◆◆

How Can I Use Colored Pencils Creatively?

The soft hues of colored pencils may be just the right touch for a special look on your pages. Their versatility will give you many options as you can see on this worksheet.

simple colorbook·········
COLOR

create a design········

color blend···
gradation···
shading···

fun template designs···
backgrounds···

PART
combine with MARKERS!

Eric and Stacy
By Carol Snyder for EK Success

The letters on this page are traced using a template. They were colored with pencils and markers — the perfect combination to duplicate the multiple colors in Stacy's dress. A sponge was used to apply color from the marker in a more muted way. After matting the main photo, draw two heavy lines around the photo and color in with the same colors of pencils and markers.

How Can I Coordinate Papers on My Pages?

There are so many different patterned papers to choose from, you won't want to limit yourself to just solid colors. You can combine prints, stripes, and polka dots − all on the same page − if you separate them with a contrasting solid color in between.

Look at how many colors and patterns have been used on the two pages shown here. Be daring! Many of the most attractive pages have unexpected combinations of paper that are coordinated creatively.

Happy Birthday Audrie
By Susan Cobb for Hot Off The Press

The birthday theme of the 8½" x 11" white patterned paper has marching critters along the bottom and has a pink ribbon border. It was matted on blue paper and then glued on a 12" x 12" red polka-dot background.

This festive page has depth and dimension added to it by using colored chalks. The balloons and letters are chalked around the edges and then glued on slightly askew to add to the liveliness of the page. The largest balloon is just right for journaling the event.

◆◆◆ coordinating ◆◆◆

Kenzi 1997
By Julie Stephani for Krause Publications

All of these different patterns in green, yellow, white, and black work great together by separating them from each other with contrasting colors. The photo of Kenzi has been matted five times with different papers, with the last black mat being cut using Scallop paper edgers. The matted photo was then glued on the bright yellow paper with the black and white dots that already had its own green-leaf border.

Kenzi's name was printed on the computer and matted before gluing onto the bottom edge of the photo mat. The whole page only took twenty minutes!

Patterned Paper

◆ ◆ ◆ vellum ◆ ◆ ◆

Can I Use a Crimper on Vellum?

Yes. It will create a lovely variation in color and will give you something new — textured vellum. The mat and hearts on this page have been crimped. Transparent mounting squares were used to adhere the dimensional pieces to the page.

Pretty in Purple
By Andrea Rothenberg for 3L

Cut photo in an oval shape, using a template or cutter. For mat, cut purple vellum, ½" larger than photo with straight-edge scissors. Run mat through crimper. Cut mat with Clouds paper edgers. Adhere photo to mat with transparent mounting squares. Adhere mat to background paper and then to white paper in same way.

Run 3" x 6" piece of purple vellum through crimper. Punch twelve hearts from crimped vellum. Group three hearts in each corner and adhere in the same way.

Shades of Color
Because vellum is transparent, it picks up the colors beneath it. See how each background paper affects the color of the yellow patterned vellum.

◆ ◆ ◆ vellum ◆ ◆ ◆

How Can I Add Vellum Accents to My Pages?

This page shows three different ways that vellum can be used: matting for photos, squares used as a border, and a square to connect the photos and dragonfly cutout accents.

Mommy's Treasures
By Shauna Berglund-Immel for Hot Off The Press

This is a beautiful combination of using vellum and collage patterned paper. The multicolored designs in the background are enhanced by the transparent vellum pieces. The dragonflies' wings are folded outward along the edge of the body to give them dimension. Simple journaling is added with a silver pen.

◆ ◆◆ vellum ◆◆◆ ◆

How Can I Use Vellum in a Different Way?

This page shows the wonderful versatility of vellum. The ability to see through it allows you to design on a page placed underneath the vellum for more creative options. Use solid or patterned paper under vellum to create an entirely new look.

Missy
By Susan Cobb for Hot Off The Press

To create the diamond pattern beneath the vellum, cut ¼ of a page from light and ¼ of a page from dark purple paper. Cut each in half diagonally. Glue two light purple pieces in opposite corners on a white background paper. Glue two dark purple pieces in the opposite corners. Glue a ¼"-wide strip of light purple paper along the inside edge of each dark purple paper. Glue ¼"-wide strip of dark purple along the inside edge of light purple paper. Place vellum over this page and glue in place where photo will cover the glue marks.

Mat the photo and journaling box with the same colors. Use a purple pen for journaling.

Yellow Roses Card
By Theresa Nelson for Hot Off The Press

Cut the yellow roses paper ½" smaller than size of card. Mat on black paper and trim to ⅛" border. Glue on card. Cut vellum ½" smaller than roses paper. Glue roses paper on at top where glue mark will be covered by rose. Cut a rose design and glue on vellum. *Option: Use foam adhesive strip to raise design above card.* Write a personal note, tuck the card into an envelope, and send it with love.

◆◆◆ vellum ◆◆◆

How Can I Adhere Vellum on My Scrapbook Pages?

Due to the translucent nature of vellum, most adhesives have a tendency to show through it. The following products will give you the best results: clear photo corners, a light coat of spray adhesive, adhesive sheets, or a Xyron machine. You can also hide adhesive behind other elements on the page such as photos, journaling boxes, die cuts, and stickers.

Family Christmas
Designed for Memory Makers

Vellum was used to create a dimensional scene by layering it over solid colored paper. It was used for the background behind the tree, the tree trimmings, and as package wrapping. The solid colors underneath show through, giving the holiday scene depth.

◆◆◆ paper tearing ◆◆◆

How Can Torn Paper Be Used on My Pages?

When you want the look of something homespun or "natural," torn paper will do the trick! It adds texture and interest to the page.

Addie's Apple Crisp

By Stacy Julian for Creating Keepsakes magazine

Mat the photo on white, then patterned, then white paper. Use the computer to type the recipe, title, and journaling. Mat the title and journaling boxes on green paper. Tear around recipe and mat on tan paper. Tear around tan paper and mat on green paper.

Stamp a large apple and leaves. Color with chalk and tear around them. Punch out three small apples and color the stems green. Position pieces on two pages. Glue in place.

◆◆◆ paper quilting ◆◆◆

How Can I Adapt a Design to Fit Large or Small Pages?

The key to changing a design to fit either an 8½" x 11" or 12" x 12" size page is changing the size of the borders. You will not be able to duplicate the exact same layout, but you will be able to achieve the same look.

You Are My Sunshine
Designed for Memory Makers

The center of both pages has the same layout of photos and designs. The only difference is the borders. The smaller page has a border along the bottom edge only. The larger page has narrower borders on all four sides. The secret was creating an 8½" wide center section.

The basic grid is made up of nine scant 2⅞" squares. Four smaller 2" squares are placed on end to create a quilted look.

How Can I Bring Nature Onto My Pages?

The easiest way is to select patterned papers that have designs from nature. When choosing accents, use punches, stamps, die cuts, and stickers in plant and wildlife motifs.

Maggie & Eddie

By Andrea Rothenberg for Delta Technical Coatings

Create your own leaf background paper using stamps and acid-free paper paint. Apply paint to the stamps with a sponge, using only one color of paint or using several colors blended right on the stamp. Stamp several leaves on a separate piece of paper and cut out. Use leaves as dimensional accents on the page.

The Metz's
Ron, Carole and
Annie
September 1999

The Metz's

By Julie McGuffee for Kodak

A leaf-print background paper is perfect for this family portrait taken outdoors. Coordinating colored papers add to the overall effect. The punched-out leaves in the matting add a nice touch, especially when one leaf is added as an accent in the journaling box, too. Photo corners were used for both the photo and journaling, which was printed on the computer using a matching colored type.

◆ ◆ ◆ tea-bag folding ◆ ◆ ◆

How Can I Use Tea Bag Folding on My Pages?

This popular technique of folding small squares of patterned paper can be used as a special unique design element on your pages. Use papers that will coordinate well with the rest of the page. Tea-bag folding is so much fun to do!

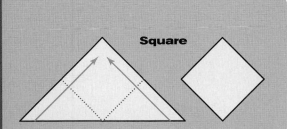

Square

Note: 1½" squares were used for the design shown.

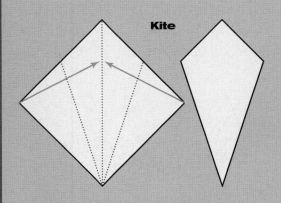

Kite

Basic Folds

Square fold: Cut a square in half diagonally. Turn it right side down with its long side toward you. Fold each side point to the top. Turn right side up.

Kite fold: Fold a square in half diagonally one way and then the other to find the center. Place it right side down and fold each side in to lie against the center line. Turn the kite right side up.

Kim

By Amy Gustafson for Hot Off The Press

Learn to fold two simple shapes to create the dimensional star on this page. Begin by folding eight roses squares into "kite" shapes. Lay them on black paper with long points joining in center. Fold eight peach filigree squares into "kite" shapes and insert them underneath the rose kites, having the long points of rose kites facing out. Glue in place. Cut around design, leaving a black ⅛" mat. For center, cut one peach square in half diagonally and fold into small square. Glue in center of star.

Cut the corners of the photos with decorative scissors. Cut out roses and glue into two of the spaces. The matting and confetti die cut pick up the colors in the tea-bag folded star.

◆◆◆ pop-ups ◆◆◆

How Can I Make a Pop-Up Page in My Scrapbook?

Adding dimension to your pages is easy with pop-ups. They require a hinged base that fits between two pages. The base is glued to the pages, and the items that will pop up are attached to the base. Choose from these three styles of boxes.

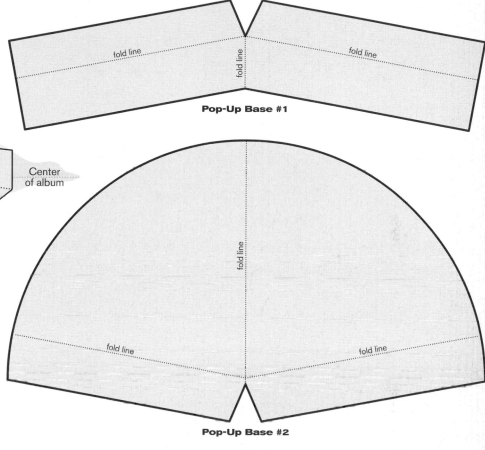

Pop-Up Base #1

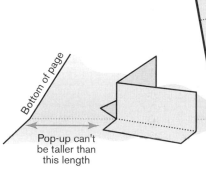

Bottom of page

Center of album

Pop-up can't be taller than this length

Pop-Up Basics

1 Enlarge pop-up base pattern to needed size. Cut base from card stock.

2 Fold in half. Fold bottom edges up.

3 Glue bottom folds on two scrapbook pages at 45-degree angles, one half on each side of center. Close pages to check position.

4 Glue items on pop-up base. Be sure the items are not taller than the distance between the bottom of the page and the center fold of base. See illustration.

Pop-Up Base #2

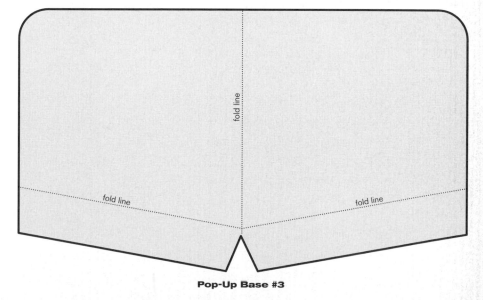

Pop-Up Base #3

Happy Birthday Pop-Up
By Debra Jennis for Accu-Cut

Cut two pop-up bases #2 and one base #1 from card stock, using the patterns on the previous page or a die and the die-cutting system. Cut the top of one base #2 off 1" above fold line. Glue it back on, having bottom edge at fold line. Cut multi-color letters, balloons, gift packages, and confetti die cuts. Glue "Happy" letters on taller base and "Birthday" letters on shorter base. Glue balloons on ends of five confetti pieces. Glue confetti ends on back of letters. Glue five confetti pieces on base #1.

Cut ½" off top and one side of two pieces of white card stock. Glue on two pieces of turquoise card stock. Glue bases on pages in graduating order, having taller base at top of page.

Crop photos. Trim gift package die-cuts to frame photos. Glue photos on packages and then on page. Glue confetti on page. Print title and journaling. Make small dots all over page with turquoise marker.

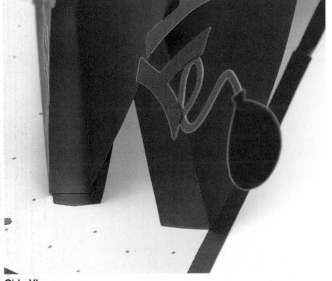

Side View

◆ ◆◆ ◆ pop-ups ◆ ◆◆ ◆

Halloween Pop-Up
By Julie McGuffee for Accu-Cut

Cut pop-up bases #1 (dark green) and #2 (bright yellow) from card stock using the patterns on the previous page or a die and the die-cutting system. Extend length of #1 base 3" on each side of fold. Cut the following die-cuts: black house, cat; bright green grass, large & small trees; dark green small tree; yellow moon, orange pumpkin, 2 white ghosts. Cut tombstone from gray paper. Dress Paperkin witch in costume. Glue pieces on #1 base as shown in photo. Glue large green tree on base #2, which is the moon. Glue bases on pages, having #2 base at top of page.

Crop photos. Mat on yellow paper, then orange for two photos. Cut second mat with Dragonback paper edgers. Use opposite colors for other photo. Position pieces on page. Glue in place.

Press candy-corn stickers on borders of pages. Make small dash lines connecting the candy with white opaque marker. Print title and journaling with same marker. Print "Boo" on ghosts.

Another version of the page has a tombstone card that opens up to reveal more photos!

••• dimensional folds •••

How Can I Make Dimensional Folds on My Pages?

Here are three basic folds that will give you many creative options for your pages. They will turn ordinary pages into displays with movement and pizzazz!

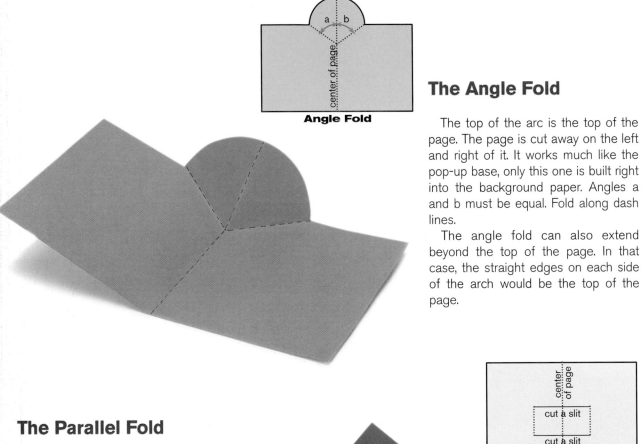

Angle Fold

The Angle Fold

The top of the arc is the top of the page. The page is cut away on the left and right of it. It works much like the pop-up base, only this one is built right into the background paper. Angles a and b must be equal. Fold along dash lines.

The angle fold can also extend beyond the top of the page. In that case, the straight edges on each side of the arch would be the top of the page.

The Parallel Fold

This fold is cut horizontally across the center of two pages. It can be positioned higher or lower on the page than shown. Points a and b must be equal, but they can be of any length. The width between the lines can vary, but the horizontal cuts must be the same lengths.

Use a craft knife to cut a slit along two solid lines indicated. Fold along dash lines.

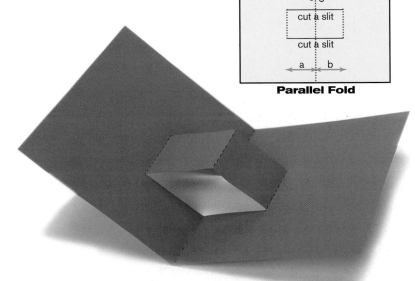

Parallel Fold

◆ ◆ ◆ dimensional folds ◆ ◆ ◆

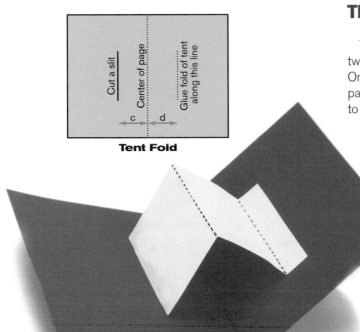

Tent Fold

Labels in diagram: Cut a slit · Center of page · Glue fold of tent along this line · c · d

The Tent Fold

The tent is a separate piece that extends over two pages and has one end attached to each page. On the tent piece, a and b must be equal. On the page, c and d must be equal. In order for the tent to move correctly, a-b must be greater than c-d.

Use a craft knife to cut a slit along solid line indicated. Fold tent along dash lines. The dotted line indicates position of the fold of the tent. Glue in place. Insert tab in slit. Glue in place.

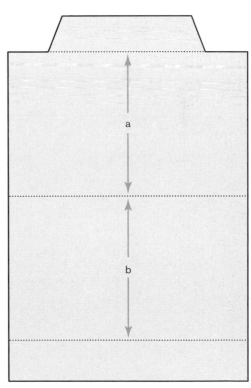

Fold-Out Tips

◆ The fold-out portion of the page can not be contained in a protective plastic sheet. Once you've completed your page, measure the base of the fold-out and mark this on the plastic sheet. Cut out just the top layer of the plastic. Insert your page into the sleeve.

◆ People will enjoy manipulating the action of the fold-out, so glue pieces securely.

◆ Design your page and position all of the elements before gluing anything in place. Glue the pieces on the bottom layer first if any items overlap.

◆ Use fold-outs selectively throughout your albums. The extra cardstock and elements will add weight and bulkiness.

◆ Once you become comfortable using fold-outs, be creative! Change the shapes to fit your personal needs. Use them to enhance your special theme pages.

Tent Pattern

Labels in diagram: a · b

How Can I Make a Photo Wheel?

All you need is a common paper fastener. Insert it through the top circle and then into the background paper. Spread the fastener on the back of the page and spin the circle on the front to see all of the photos!

Turn the wheel to see all four photos.

Paper Fastener

Audrie
By Lenae Gerig for Hot Off The Press

You only see one picture of Audrie at a time, but there are four photos of her on this page. The opening in the circle reveals them as you spin it around. Begin by cropping four photos in 2¾" circles. Place them on a 7½" circle cut from white paper with Wave paper edgers. Press stickers on paper in space between photos.

For wheel, cut a 6¾" circle from patterned paper using same edgers. Cut 2" circle opening on one side. Mat on pink card stock and trim a scant border on outside edge using same edgers. Trim a scant border around 2" circle with straight-edge scissors.

Center wheel on white circle and align photos underneath so they can be seen easily through opening. Glue photos in place. Insert paper fastener through center of wheel and through center of white circle. Spread fastener on the back of page.

Use stencil to trace letters with pink marker. Cut around letters, leaving a scant border around ink marks. Glue letters on wheel, substituting a sticker for one letter. For corners, cut four triangles from patterned paper. Cut long edges with Wave paper edgers. Mat on white paper and trim a scant border. Glue a triangle on each corner.

Arrange four photos underneath the wheel

◆◆◆ movement ◆◆◆

How Can I Make Something Animated on My Pages?

Use the same method as with the wheel on the previous page. Use a paper fastener to create a moveable joint like Pooh's arm on the page shown here.

Pooh waves his flag.

Molly on the Carousel
By Lenae Gerig for Hot Off The Press

Cut out a character like Pooh bear and cut a separate arm. Insert the paper fastener into the arm, then into the body. Spread the fastener on the back side of the body. Note: Use card stock to make the moveable arm more durable. Use a ⅛" circle punch to make holes in which to insert the fastener.

Mat photos on gold, then pink paper, trimming to ⅛" borders. Cut a heart from lavender paper and mat on pink paper, trimming to ⅛" border. Position pieces on page and glue in place.

◆◆◆ movement ◆◆◆

How Can I Make a Slide on My Page?

You can make a slide with just one strip of paper! Cut a slit in your page where you want the slide to go. You will be surprised at how many things you'll find that can move across your pages, adding interest and fun.

Pull a cutout shape across the page.

Basic Slide

1 Cut a narrow slit in background paper where you want slide to go.

2 Cut slide pattern from card stock. Fold to back along two center fold lines. Fold to front along two outer fold lines.

3 Insert slide into slit in paper with folds in front and ends in back.

4 Glue object on top of front of slide.

5 Pull object back and forth on slide. **Option:** *Glue a strip of paper on back of object for a pull tab.*

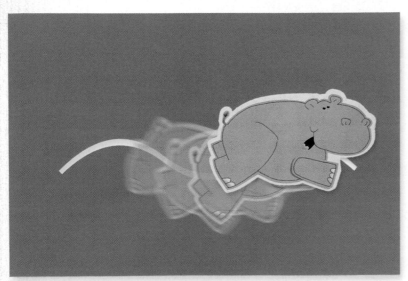

Cut a curvy line for a more animated movement.

Slider Front

Slider Back

fold lines   fold lines

Slide Platform

Mickey at Blizzard Beach
By Susan Cobb for Hot Off The Press

Mat photos on gold then blue paper, trimming them to ⅛" borders. Use the Wave paper edgers to cut edges of waves in parallel lines from the following card stock: white, blue, turquoise, white. With craft knife, cut a narrow slit, following the line of the waves.

Cut out Mickey and punch out Pluto. Use pattern to cut out a slide platform from white card stock. Fold platform and insert it into slit with folds in front and ends in back. Glue Mickey on top of slide platform.

Position pieces on background paper and glue in place, keeping glue away from platform and slit of slide. Print journaling on white wave with blue marker.

Pull Mickey down the water slide!

How Can I Use Pull Tabs to Add Journaling on My Pages?

When there isn't enough room on your page to add the journaling you want to . . . just make more room. One way is to use a pull tab that is hidden behind one of the photos and pulls out to reveal more journaling.

Front

Back (Vellum was used for rectangle cover to show journaling slide inside.)

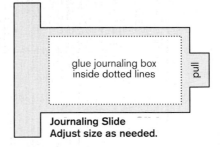

glue journaling box
inside dotted lines

pull

Journaling Slide
Adjust size as needed.

The Reunion

By Julie Stephani for Krause Publications

My page was already full with five photos on it, but I wanted to include the names of everyone in the group photo who attended the reunion. By including a pull tab hidden behind the photo, I could do it!

Pull Tab

Cut the Journaling Slide from a paper that coordinates with your page. Adjust the size to accommodate journaling and to fit behind a photo. Cut a piece of white paper (or color of choice) for journaling. Journal on paper and glue paper on slide. Write "Pull" on tab. Use craft knife to cut a slit in page close to edge of photo. Insert slide. Cut a rectangle large enough to cover slide, leaving enough room to glue along three edges without interfering with movement of slide. Glue in place.

Kimberly & Michael

By Julie Stephani for Krause Publications

This is such a pretty page, but it doesn't have much room for journaling on it. I wanted to include the important information, so I made a pull-tab for the journaling and hid it behind the photo. The perfect solution!

I cut out around some of the lacy pattern on the page and inserted the bottom of the large photo under it. Then I punched out six hearts for each of the flowers and added small circles for the flower centers.

Pull the tab for more journaling details.

◆◆◆ templates ◆◆◆

How Can I Make a Border Using a Template?

It is so easy when you have a pattern to trace around. All you have to do is choose the color of pen and add details. This page is extra easy because a Plan-a-Page template was used to create the layout.

Fun in the Sun
By Beth Reames for EK Success

Create a border by tracing around the outside edge of a Beach Border Buddy. Make stripes to the outside of the page. Use the Plan-a-Page template to cut photos and arrange them on the page. Use a sun punch to add interest to the letters of the title. A teardrop punch is perfect to create the "splashes" around the page. Add journaling and doodles.

Border templates come in a variety of themes.

◆ ◆ ◆ templates ◆ ◆ ◆

How Can I Use a Template for Journaling?

Use a pencil to lightly trace around the shape and draw lines for lettering. Print journaling with a pen or marker. When ink is dry, erase pencil lines.

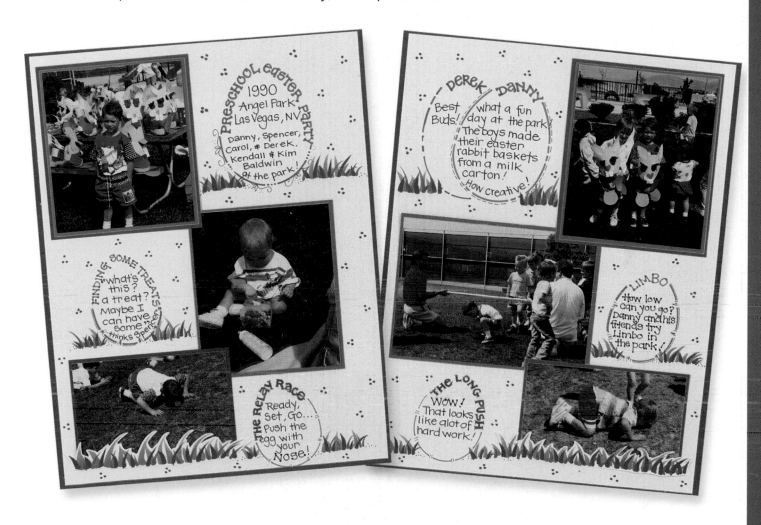

The Great Egg Race
By Carol Snyder for EK Success

Ovals are great for journaling, too! Mat photos and arrange on page, leaving room for journaling "eggs." Trace around an egg-shape template with a pencil. Trace shape with marker, leaving a space open at the top for journaling. Use larger end of a Writer marker for each title and journal inside each egg using the finer tip.

Create grass using several green shades of Scroll & Brush markers. Lay the brush end on its side and flick it up to create a great grass look. Make triple dots with the larger end of an orange Writer. Erase pencil lines.

◆◆◆ pockets ◆◆◆

How Can I Create More Room on My Pages?

One way is to attach a pocket to your page. Any shape can be used to make a pocket as long as you can glue the sides and bottom closed, leaving an opening at the top. Glue close to the edges to allow more room inside the pocket for notes, journaling, and memorabilia. Use coordinating paper so the pocket fits into the style of the page.

You can also attach the pocket to the back of your page as shown below. Create a special reminder on the front of the page to indicate that there is additional journaling attached.

Back of Page

Crystal Lake High School
By Julie Stephani for Krause Publications

This page features fairly large photos, leaving little room for journaling. Placing a pocket on the back of the page is an opportunity to include several pages of written memories as well as memorabilia. The small labeled arrow on the page indicates that there is journaling attached.

◆ ◆ ◆ pockets ◆ ◆ ◆

Grandma's Brag Book

By Barb Lashua for Fiskars

Punch a flower design in each corner of photo. Mat photo on tan paper and trim to ⅛" border with Deckle paper edgers. Mat again on gray/blue paper and trim to ⅛" border with straight-edge scissors. Cut a large triangle for pocket from patterned paper, cutting only two sides with same edgers. Punch two circles ¾" apart four times along long edge for ribbon. Insert ribbon. Glue ends down and tie in a bow at center. Mat on blue/gray paper and trim to ⅛" border. Glue photo and pocket on page.

For book, cut four (or as many as you like) 3½" squares. For cover, cut 3" square from patterned paper, using same edgers. Mat on blue/gray paper and cut with same edger. Glue on cover. Use computer to print title and journaling. Cut a rectangle around type. Punch a teddy bear in each corner. Mat on blue/gray paper and trim closely. Glue title on cover and journaling on pocket. Insert a fabric eyelet in one corner of each square, following the package instructions. Crop photos into 3" squares. Punch corners with different small shapes. Mat on different colors and trim closely. Glue on front and back of squares. Insert 10" length of ¼" ribbon into eyelets. Tie pages together in a bow. Insert book into pocket.

◆◆◆ envelopes ◆◆◆

How Can I Use Envelopes on My Pages?

Make any size envelope to hold notes, journaling, or memorabilia on your page. Enlarge or reduce pattern to the size you need. Make envelopes from papers that coordinate with the other elements on your page.

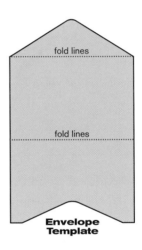

Envelope Template

Enlarge or reduce pattern to the size you need

My Prom

By Julie Stephani for Krause Publications

The matting around the photo looks like the lighter patterned paper has been cut with decorative scissors on the inside and outside. Actually, the photo was matted on white paper cut to ⅛" with a straight-edge scissor. Next it was matted on purple paper cut with Victorian paper edgers, then matted on the lighter patterned paper, and was parallel cut with the same scissors as the purple mat. It was then matted on purple paper cut to ¼" with a straight-edge scissors, which was repeated on white paper.

◆◆◆ envelopes ◆◆◆

Best Friends

By Julie Stephani for Krause Publications

Envelopes can come in all sizes! These fun little envelopes hold small notes and special information. They are labeled so you know what is inside. Don't be afraid to include a page that is all journaling. Sometimes it is just as important as the photos.

◆◆◆ memorabilia ◆◆◆

How Can I Include Memorabilia On My Pages?

Use acid-free, archival-safe clear plastic pockets to include special dimensional keepsakes in your memory albums. They will store and preserve your treasures, prevent acid-transfer, and keep important memories from being lost.

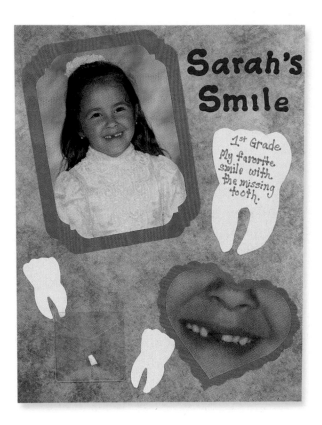

Sarah's Smile
By Andrea Rothenberg for 3L

Capture the big day when a child loses his or her first tooth! Take photos, including a close-up, so you can see the space where it was. Place the tooth in a plastic pocket to save it for a keepsake.

Newspaper clippings have a high acidity. Laminate them to keep acid migration from harming photos they may touch.

Massi Warrior
By Andrea Rothenberg for 3L

Plastic pockets come in different sizes, so choose the one that best fits your keepsakes. Include one or more on a page, adhering them directly to the background paper or sticking them on a mat first.

The adhesive on the flap is repositionable, so keepsakes can be taken out to look at and then can be placed back in the pocket and resealed. The adhesive on the back of the pocket is transparent and will stick permanently to the page.

How Can I Turn Color Photos Into Black & Whites?

You may want black and white photos for a special effect on your pages or so you can color tint them. A colored photo that has a good contrast of lights and darks will reproduce best. Use the Kodak Picturemaker and choose the black & white option. You can also turn a color or black & white photo into a sepia (brown tone) photo.

McGuffee
David Martin
Born - May 31, 1979
Fort Worth, Texas

McGuffee
Jennifer Diane
Born - Nov 13, 1975
Ramstein, Germany

Original Photos

McGuffee Babies
By Julie McGuffee for Kodak

This is a good example of when you may want to turn a color photo into a black & white one. Julie wanted to have pictures of both of her children on the same page, but one photo was color and one was black & white. She simply changed the color photo to black & white to match the other one.

The patterned strip of paper arranged diagonally across the page is the perfect elegant background to enhance the delicate lacy scherenschnitte frames. An additional touch of color was added to the frames and floral cutouts using chalk.

◆◆◆ Photos ◆◆◆

How Can Photographs Be Easily Enlarged?

There are many times when you want to enlarge a photo, or even a certain portion of a photo. This is easy to do on the Kodak Picturemaker. Simply scan the photo and follow the prompts on the screen to zoom in on the portion of the photo you would like to enlarge. Enlargements can be made up to 8"x10".

Alex Bay
By Julie McGuffee for Kodak

Original Photo

See how small the dog in the boat looked in the original photo? To make sure the dog would be seen on the scrapbook page, the photo was enlarged and the scenery around the boat was cropped out.

The photos were used as guides in choosing the design of the page. The striped paper duplicates the parallel lines of the wooden dock, and the bold strips reflect the many posts and poles in the photos. The strips connect the photos and journaling to each other vertically. The corners of the photos and mats at the center of the page are also layered to connect the photos horizontally.

Note how a photograph of a sign serves as a title, and a computer was used to add some additional details.

◆◆◆ Photos ◆◆◆

How Can I Remove Red Eye from Photos?

Using a flash on your camera can often cause the eye pupils to turn bright red in our photographs. This can be easily fixed by using the "red eye removal" feature on the Kodak Picturemaker found at your local store.

You can also use a "red-eye remover" pen to change the eye pupil back to its normal color. Sometimes an animal's eyes will turn yellow or green instead of red. Then use a "pet eye" pen.

1 Place a photo on the screen.

2 Follow the user-friendly prompts.

3 Pick up your finished photos.

Romeo Album
By Julie McGuffee for Kodak

This could have been a photo that you wouldn't want to use, but with the help of the red-eye remover option on the Kodak Picturemaker, the photo was saved. It was even enlarged and was then silhouetted to be used on the album cover.

Original Photo

Two 1" wide strips were cut from corrugated wave paper and glued on the top and bottom of the album. A 1¾" strip was glued across the center. The photo was glued in place and red heart punches were used to add accents to the album and its title. Black dots in groups of three were added as the final accents.

It Is As Easy as 1 2 3

The Kodak Picturemaker will reprint, enlarge, crop, restore color, change color, fix red eye, and more. Turn photos to sepia tone or colored photos to black and white. Create a frame or print a message right on the photo. Print photos in a variety of sizes, including several different sizes all at one time. Print digital photos in minutes.

How Can I Tint My Black and White Photos?

Use Photo Twin markers to color your photos in soft natural hues. First make a color copy of your black and white photo. A black and white copy won't give you the same subtle shades as in the original photo.

If you would like more intense color, add with light layers, letting the color dry between applications. Practice with the markers on white paper before coloring photo.

Color with light layers.

Ellen and Marjorie
By Carol Snyder for EK Success

A color copy of the original black and white photo was used for this page. The photo was matted with two thin solid colors. The larger mat was created by tracing around a border template. The journaling box was matted with coordinating colors.

How Can I Capture the Look of Vintage Photos?

Reprints of old black and white photographs can be made using the black and white option on the Kodak Picturemaker. However, if you would like to maintain the warmth of the old photos, make your reprints using the color option. It will duplicate the original tones and will even pick up some of the aging details to make them look truly vintage on your page. It is also possible to turn both color and black and white photos into sepia (brown tone) prints by making that selection on the option menu.

Original

Black & White Copy

The Turners
By Julie McGuffee for Kodak

How you choose to reprint your old photos will make a difference. These original photos were reprinted in color in order to capture their vintage look. See one of the original photos and its black and white reprint to make the comparison.

The photos on the left were matted on parchment paper first, but note how the bottom one has the parchment rectangle that is the same size as the photo centered horizontally beneath it. The photo on the right has a black rectangle the same size as the photo and was glued at an angle. The paper with the collection of old stamps adds to the nostalgic feel of the page.

How Can I Use Instant Photos on My Page?

It is recommended that you do not cut instant photos, so you may want to make a reprint of them in order to do some creative cropping. Using the Kodak Picturemaker will also give you the option of cropping photos before they are reprinted, giving you larger images. Older photos that may have lost some of the original color can also be restored and the color balance can be adjusted if necessary. Even "red eye" problems can be corrected.

Original Photos

Christmas 1982
By Julie McGuffee for Kodak

You can see how Julie's instant photos from the past have been improved by cropping and enlarging them for her scrapbook page. The original images were only 3½" square, but the 3½" x 5" reprints are a much better size for the 12" x 12" page. The unnecessary backgrounds have been cropped away, and the focus is on the children and kitten. Picking up the bright yellow from the ball in the photo adds a nice additional color to the traditional red and green of Christmas.

◆ ◆ ◆ photos ◆ ◆ ◆

How Can I Adjust Photo Sizes?

When you are doing a grouping of photos, you may want to adjust some photos so they are uniform in size. You can do this by making color copies and either enlarging or reducing the size before printing. You can also use the Kodak Picturemaker and change the sizes of photos by either cropping them or selecting a different picture size before printing.

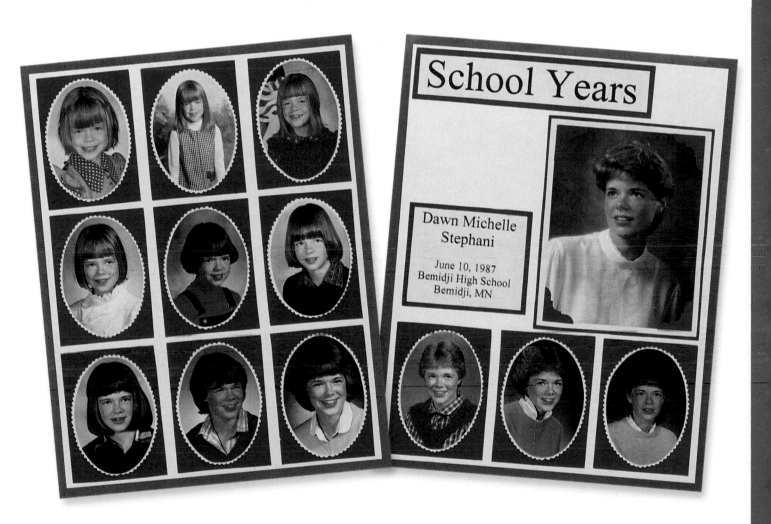

Dawn's Graduation
By Julie Stephani for Krause Publications

In order to do this composite of my daughter's class pictures, I needed to change some of the sizes of photos to make them uniform. I chose not to change one photo because I didn't want to crop out a special outfit that she was wearing. It was easy to enlarge and reduce the photos on a copy machine to get them the sizes I wanted.

In order to fit twelve photos on one page, I created a grid. I kept the matting simple since I had so many photos to do. Each small photo was matted on white, and the scant border was cut with a Mini Scallop paper edgers. Then it was matted on a blue rectangle.

◆◆◆ dimension ◆◆◆

How Can I Create 3-D Photos?

Create dynamic dimensional photos that you will want to frame! They can be placed in your albums when you are ready to retire them to make ready for new photos. The process isn't as difficult as it may first appear.

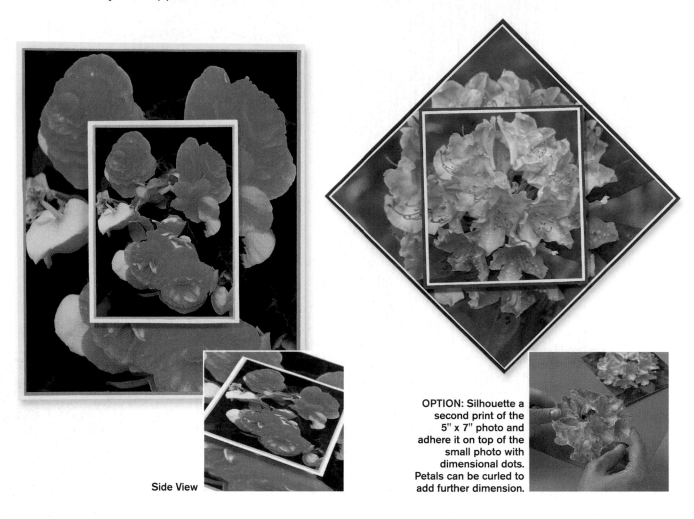

Side View

OPTION: Silhouette a second print of the 5" x 7" photo and adhere it on top of the small photo with dimensional dots. Petals can be curled to add further dimension.

Yellow Begonias
By Julie Stephani for Krause Publications

This combination requires photos size 4" x 6" and 8" x 10". Mat both photos the same. Mat photo on lime green paper and trim to ⅛" border. Mat on white card stock and trim to ¼" border. Adhere nine dimensional dots on back of small matted photo. Remove protective papers from each dot and press photo on center of large photo.

Pink Rhododendron
By Julie Stephani for Krause Publications

This combination requires photos size 5" x 7" and 8" x 10". Crop small photo to 5" x 5½". (This photo would probably look better if it was square, but I couldn't part with the extra ½" of pretty petals!) Crop large photo to 8" x 8". Mat small photo on white paper and trim to ⅛" border. Mat on green card stock and trim to ⅛" border. Mat large photo on white paper and trim to ⅛" border. Mat on black card stock and trim to ¼" border. Adhere nine dimensional dots on back of small matted photo. Remove protective papers from each dot and press photo on center of large photo.

◆•◆ ◆•◆ dimension ◆◆◆ ◆◆◆

Side View

Tiger Lillies
By Julie Stephani for Krause Publications

This combination requires two 8" x 10" photos. Mat photo on yellow paper and trim to ⅛" border. Mat on green card stock and trim to ¼" border. Silhouette several flowers from the group, selecting the ones that appear closer to the camera. Cut slits between petals to separate them. Curl petals gently around finger. Adhere dimensional dots on back of flowers. Remove protective papers from each dot and press each flower on base photo, directly over their duplicate image.

Dimensional Photo Basics

1 Make duplicates of your photos. You may need different sizes, depending on the design.

2 Use a swivel craft knife to make cuts within the photo.

3 Use dimensional foam dots or strips to raise the cut pieces above the base photo.

◆◆◆ dimension ◆◆◆

Can Photos of People Be Made 3-D, Too?

Of course they can! Every photo will not be a good candidate, but many photos will become dynamic when you give them an added dimension.

Duplicates of photos are needed to cut out the areas that you want raised above the rest of the photo. Select the objects that are closest to the camera. You can even add more than one level. The boys with the ball are raised up off of the background, and the ball is raised up off of them.

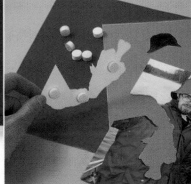

Foam dots add dimension.

Nicholas
By Julie Stephani for Krause Publications

Two 5" x 7" photos were used for this dimensional picture. A swivel craft knife was used to cut the hat and the arm holding the fish out of one photo. Adhere dimensional dots on back of cut pieces. Remove protective papers from each dot and press on base photo, directly over their duplicate images.

Mat photo on lime gold paper, using red photo corners and trim to ⅛" border. Mat on blue paper and trim to ½" border. Mat on white card stock, using red photo corners and trim to ⅛" border.

◆◆◆ dimension ◆◆◆

Side View

Side View

Having a Ball
By Julie Stephani for Krause Publications

Three 5" x 7" photos were used for this dimensional picture. A swivel craft knife was used to cut the boys out of one photo and the ball and hands out of another. Adhere dimensional dots on back of cut pieces. Remove protective papers from each dot and press on base photo, directly over their duplicate images. The boys were adhered first, then the ball.

Mat photo on lime green paper and trim to ¼" border. Cut white mat same size as green mat. Offset it on one side of green mat, leaving a ¼" border. Mat on yellow card stock and trim to ¼" border. Use black marker to make dots and wavy lines around white mat.

Jacob At Work
By Julie Stephani for Krause Publications

Two 5" x 7" photos were used for this dimensional picture. A swivel craft knife was used to cut the boy and bulldozer out of one photo. Adhere dimensional dots on back of cut pieces. Remove protective papers from each dot and press on base photo, directly over their duplicate images.

Mat 5½" x 7½" blue paper on white paper and trim scant border with Mini Pinking paper edgers. Mat on yellow card stock and trim to ¼" border. Glue photo on mat at an angle.

◆ ◆ ◆ panoramic ◆ ◆ ◆

How Can I Use Panoramic Photos On My Pages?

It can be done, but you need to be a little creative! You will either have to cut the photo into sections or extend your page to fit the longer size. Placing them vertically on the page will help or just place them on a 12" x 12" page. You can extend your page by attaching two pages together with strip hinges glued onto the back of the pages. Place the top piece outside the protective sleeve, so it can be opened up.

4904 Daniel Drive

Three separate photos give a panoramic view.

Stephani Back Yard

By Julie Stephani for Krause Publications

When we were moving from Illinois, I wanted to capture the whole back yard, but I didn't have a panoramic camera – so I improvised. I took three separate photos holding my camera at the same level. I started on the left side and panned (moved) the camera to the right each time, making sure that each subsequent photo had the left side of the frame overlapping the right side of the previous frame. Then I cropped them to fit perfectly and placed them very close to each other on my scrapbook page. It gives the feeling of seeing the whole yard, just as if I had taken a panoramic photo.

I matched the green, black, and white in the photos when I chose my matting papers. For a title, I die cut the letters from a strip of black paper and used the negative space rather than the letters themselves. I used chalk to add just a little shading inside the letters.

◆◆◆ panoramic ◆◆◆

August 10-12, 2000

Sequoia and Kings Canyon

Two separate photos give a panoramic view

The Sequoia

By Julie Stephani for Krause Publications

When we visited the Sequoia National Park and Kings Canyon, I knew I would have a problem capturing the huge trees and expansive scenery with my camera's limited capabilities. I solved the problem in two ways. First, I took more than one photo of the trees to get a panoramic view. I held my camera centered straight in front of me for the first picture then moved it upward, making sure that the second photo had the bottom of the frame overlapping the top of the previous frame.

The second thing that I did was buy an assortment of postcards so I could include photos taken by professional photographers on my pages. Their skills and equipment captured the scenery better than I ever could. I bought mini postcards because I had already visualized what I wanted to do on my scrapbook pages when we returned from our vacation.

I made a colored copy of a map of the park and used that for a background, and it also doubled as a hinge to hold the two 8½" x 11" pages together. Dark green photo corners were used to pick up the color of the trees. Each of the individual postcards has a description of what is in the photograph, so they can be lifted from the corners in order to read what is on the back of each one.

How Do I Add a Frame and Text on a Photo?

One way is to use the Kodak Picturemaker, which will take you through each step with easy to follow prompts on a computer screen.

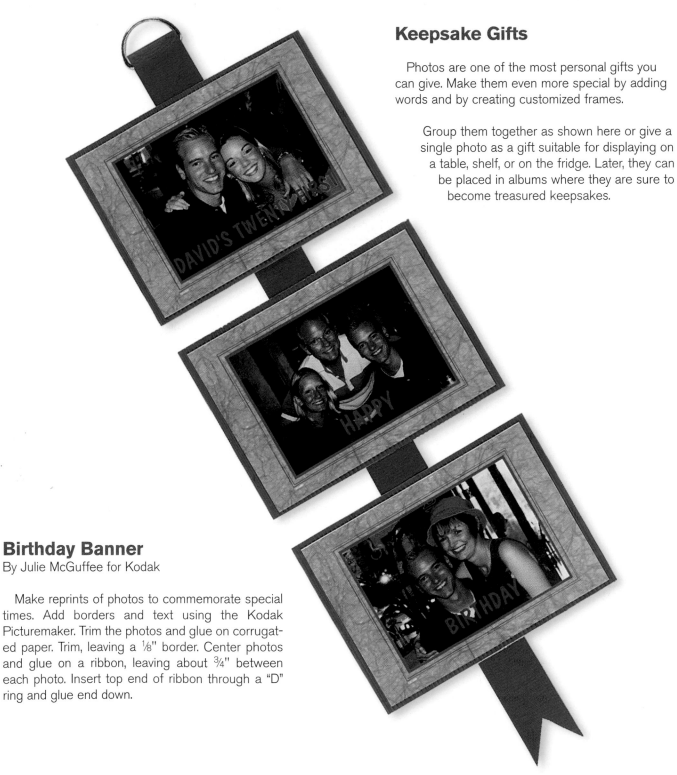

Keepsake Gifts

Photos are one of the most personal gifts you can give. Make them even more special by adding words and by creating customized frames.

Group them together as shown here or give a single photo as a gift suitable for displaying on a table, shelf, or on the fridge. Later, they can be placed in albums where they are sure to become treasured keepsakes.

Birthday Banner
By Julie McGuffee for Kodak

Make reprints of photos to commemorate special times. Add borders and text using the Kodak Picturemaker. Trim the photos and glue on corrugated paper. Trim, leaving a ⅛" border. Center photos and glue on a ribbon, leaving about ¾" between each photo. Insert top end of ribbon through a "D" ring and glue end down.

◆◆◆ software ◆◆◆

How Can I Use A Computer To Create Pages?

There are many scrapbooking software programs available for your computer. Some of them have specific themes and others have a variety of themes from which to choose. They are user friendly and will guide you through custom making pages for your individual needs.

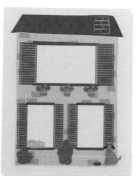

The page as it was printed.

The Stephani Family
By Julie Stephani for Krause Publications

The program used for this page offers themed pages and backgrounds that can be changed to fit the photos. In this case, the window sizes were adjusted as well as repositioned. The journaling was easily typed in and placed where it was needed. The bottom of the page was "bumped" out and matted on turquoise paper, which was cut with Wave paper edgers. Windows were cut out and photos inserted behind each opening. Then the piece was glued on the brown background paper.

◆◆◆ scanning ◆◆◆

How Can I Use My Computer for Creating Backgrounds?

Make your own custom and creative backgrounds using your home computer, a scanner, and a printer. Look at the pages shown here as examples. Baby pins were scanned for the perfect baby shower background. What could be more perfect than jelly beans as a theme for the birthday party on the next page? The best part was that the pages were created at home with items on hand.

Kyle Thomas
By Barbara Kotsos for Epson

Two photos were matted on gold paper and trimmed to ¼" borders. The other photo is silhouetted and matted with blue paper and trimmed to ¼ border. Design elements were printed from the computer software program. The birth certificate was copied using the scanner and then matted on blue paper and trimmed the same as photos. Four 1"-wide baby-blue strips create the border on each page. Gold 1" squares are glued on in each corner. A small photo "sticker" was added next to the journaling.

Scatter objects randomly on the screening bed. Close the lid and print.

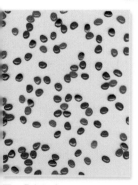

The Printed Background Paper

Justin's 10th Birthday

By Barbara Kotsos for Epson

The bright jelly-bean background paper created using the scanner sets the mood for this fun page. The one main photo dominates the page and is matted on red paper and trimmed to a ½" border. Wave paper edgers were used to cut the gold ½" border strips. The title and journaling were printed from the computer and then cut into shapes. A red cord is tied into a bow and hangs from the balloon. The journaling box is matted on red and then gold and trimmed to ¼" borders.

◆◆◆ borders ◆ ◆ ◆

How Can I Use My Computer for Creating Borders and Frames?

Use computer software clip art to create personalized frames and borders to set off your photos and pages. Customize designs, colors, and sizes to create a page that will carry the theme through from top to bottom.

Blue Mountain Lake
By Barbara Kotsos for Epson

This is a perfect example of how the theme is carried throughout the page. The fish and lure clip art is used in the title, as design elements on the page, in the photo mats, and on the page borders. The sizes can vary to fit your needs. The backgrounds are changed from dark green to yellow to keep the page interesting, so it doesn't look too repetitive. The type font fits the style of the page, and the small sticker photos add a nice touch.

Here are some of the elements that went into this page . . .

Scanned Photo

Background Paper

Frame

Be Mine!

By Barbara Kotsos for Epson

Software clip art was used to create this page. First, the photo was scanned in to duplicate the original. Then clip art was chosen for the background design and was customized with choice of color and the couples' names. It was printed out in a repeating pattern by copying it onto the whole page. A frame was selected and the photo was inserted into it.

◆◆◆ journaling ◆◆◆

How Can I Use My Computer for Journaling?

You can get many of the same results with the computer as you can when you write titles and journal by hand – and in a fraction of the time.

Christmas
By Barbara Kotsos for Epson

Computer software programs offer a great choice in different lettering styles called "fonts." Some of the advantages of using a computer are getting a consistent look and a bigger variety of lettering styles. It is also easy to correct writing errors, and you can match the font style to the design theme of your pages.

A "holly" font was selected for the title. Journaling was done in white type on a green background and was then cut out in the shape of a tree. Even the Christmas list and "ho-ho-ho's" on the page were printed using the computer.

The photos are cut in a variety of shapes and matted on red or green paper and trimmed to ⅛" borders. The page borders are created with 1"-wide strips that are cut to leave the corners open for inserting a holly design. Small photo "stickers" add the final touch.

◆◆◆ transfers ◆◆◆

How Can I Use My Computer to Create Photo Transfers?

Take one of your favorite photos and transfer it onto clothing that you would be proud to wear anywhere – using your home computer and printer. The end result will be a customized garment with a photo of someone you love on it.

"Welcome Baby" T-Shirt
By Barbara Kotsos for Epson

Scan photo into your computer. Add personalized text by using the word processing application. Scan as 360 dpi and print on Ink Jet Paper to check the correct resolution of the photo. *IMPORTANT: Select "Flip Horizontal" in the printer drive to print out onto transfer paper backwards for a mirror image.* Insert one sheet of transfer paper into the printer. Print the image. Trim around the image, leaving a ¼" border.

Place a pillowcase over the fabric and press with a very hot iron with no steam. This is a very brief explanation of the process, but follow the very specific instructions included with the transfer paper.

Shirt can be washed inside out in cold water in the machine. Dry as you would any T-shirt.

"More Cookies" Apron
By Barbara Kotsos for Epson

You can iron an image on an apron in just minutes, and it's sure to be Grandma's favorite gift. Read the brief instructions for the T-shirt given here so you understand the process, but follow the very specific instructions included with the transfer paper.

◆◆◆ labels ◆◆◆

Can I Use My Computer for Creating Gift Wrap, Tags, and Labels?

Yes, you can customize personalized gift wrap, package tags, and labels – that even include photos!

Kevin Gift Wrap
By Barbara Kotsos for Epson

Enter photo into your computer using a digital flash card, a scanner, a photo CD, or floppy disk. Copy the photo, making it a repeat pattern to cover the paper. Add text if you like. Print and you are ready to wrap your package.

Auntie Mae's Gift Tags & Labels
By Barbara Kotsos for Epson

Enter photo into your computer using a digital flash card, a scanner, a photo CD, or floppy disk. Type in the text. Print it on self-adhesive paper. Cut out and place tags on packages and bags. Place labels on jars of preserves!

◆◆◆ cards ◆◆◆

Can I Use My Computer to Create Photo Greeting Cards?

Any of your photos can be entered into your computer and then used to create cards with personalized graphics and text. It's easier than you think, using software programs that take you through each step.

"Hey Uncle Mike" Card
By Barbara Kotsos for Epson

There are ways to enter photos into your computer.

1 Use a digital camera that stores all of the images on a tiny flash card, which can be loaded directly into the computer.

2 If using a photo scanner, lay your photo on the scanner bed and scan it into the computer.

3 When you process your regular film, you can ask to have your photos saved onto a floppy disk, a photo CD, or even posted onto a website.

Once your photo has been saved in the computer, open your card-making software. Follow the easy-to-understand step-by-step instructions of the program to import your photo, choose card style, add text, borders, or clip art. Then print your card.

Print Photos
Insert the digital flash card into your computer to print photos on your printer.

◆◆◆ the experts ◆◆◆

Most of the content in this book was taken from the taping of More Than Memories, *the premier scrapbooking television show broadcast on public television and the Family network. Experts join hosts Julie Stephani and Julie McGuffee to share the latest tips and techniques in scrapbooking.*

Check your local Public Broadcasting Service (PBS) or Family network for the scheduling time in your area.

**Paulette Jarvey
Hot Off The Press**

**More Than Memories hosts Julie Stephani and Julie McGuffee
Krause Publications**

**Cheryl Darrow, Debra Jennis, Cj Wilson
Accu-Cut Systems**

**Barbara Kotsos, Jenny Dean
Epson America, Inc.**

the experts

Carol Snyder
EK Success

Kattia Sanchez
Eastman Kodak Company

Barb Lashua
Fiskars, Inc.

Robin Rinehart
Fiskars, Inc.

••• the experts •••

Julianna Hudgins
JANGLE.com

Host Julie and Michele Gerbrandt
Memory Makers Magazine

Deanna Lambson and Staci Julian
Creating Keepsakes Magazine

Andrea Rothenberg
Delta Technical Coatings, 3L Corporation

◆◆◆ TV taping ◆◆◆

Director Eric Steerman goes over a segment with Michele Gerbrandt, Julie McGuffee, and Julie Stephani.

Tired hosts Julie and Julie at the end of the taping.

Makeup artist Gail Tanger styles Jenny Dean's hair.

Michelle Minken and Michele Gerbrandt prepare materials for the next segment.

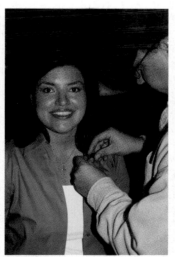

Kattia Sanchez gets "miked."

Director Eric Steerman gets a kiss from Paulette Jarvey when she finishes her segments.

glossary

Acid Free

Acid is used in paper manufacturing to break apart the wood fibers and the lignin, which holds them together. If acid remains in the materials used for photo albums, the acid can react chemically with photographs and accelerate their deterioration. Acid-free products have a pH factor of 7 to 8.5. It is imperative that all materials (glue, pens, paper, etc.) used in memory albums be acid free.

Acid Migration

The transfer of acidity from one item to another through physical contact or acidic vapors. If a newspaper clipping was put into an album, the area it touched would turn yellow or brown. A de-acidification spray can be used on acidic paper or they can be color photocopied onto acid-free papers.

Archival

A non-technical term suggesting that a material is permanent, durable, or chemically stable. It usually means that the material can safely be used for preservation purposes, although there are no quantifiable standards as to how long a material must last.

Buffered Paper

During manufacturing, a buffering agent such as calcium carbonate or magnesium bicarbonate can be added to paper to neutralize acid contaminants. Such papers have a pH of 8.5.

Cropping

Cutting or trimming a photo to keep only the most important parts.

Die

The template blade that is designed to cut a distinctive shape.

Die Cuts

Precut paper shapes used to decorate papers.

Focal Point

The emphasis in a photograph or on a page.

Journaling

Text on an album page giving details about the photographs or event. It can be handwritten, printed by computer, or can be spelled out using adhesive letters, rub-ons, etc. It is one of the most important parts of memory albums because it tells the story behind the photos.

Lignin

The bonding material that holds wood fibers together as a tree grows. If lignin remains in the final paper product (as with newsprint), it will become yellow and brittle over time. Most paper is lignin free.

Matting

Background paper used to frame and enhance the photo image.

pH Factor

Refers to the acidity of a paper. The pH scale is the standard for measurement of acidity and alkalinity. It runs from 0 to 154 with each number representing a ten-fold increase. PH neutral is 7. Acid-free products have a pH factor from 7 to 8.5. Special pH tester pens are available to help determine the acidity or alkalinity of products.

Proportion

The relationship of the parts of a layout to one another and to the page as a whole.

Photo Safe

A term similar to "archival quality" but more specific to materials used with photographs. Acid-free is the determining factor for a product to be labeled photo safe.

Sheet Protectors

Plastic sheets made to slip over a finished album page. They can be side-loading or top-loading and fit 8½" x 11½" pages or 12" x 12" pages. It is important that they be acid free. Polypropylene is commonly used.

◆◆ index ◆◆